HO GLOWS

a

COURAGEOUS

Girl

A DEVOTIONAL

HOW GOD GROWS a COURAGEOUS Girl

A DEVOTIONAL

carey scott

SHILOH ! kidz

An Imprint of Barbour Publishing, Inc.

ISBN 978-1-64352-157-2

Published by Shiloh Kidz, an imprint of Barbour Publishing, Inc., 1810 Barbour Drive, Uhrichsville, Ohio 44683, www.shilohkidz.com

Our mission is to inspire the world with the life-changing message of the Bible.

Member of the
Evangelical Christian
Publishers Association

Printed in the United States of America.

06673 0919 SP

GOD IS GROWING YOU INTO A COURAGEOUS GIRL!

"Be strong and have strength of heart. Do not be afraid or shake with fear because of them. For the Lord your God is the One Who goes with you. He will be faithful to you. He will not leave you alone."
DEUTERONOMY 31:6

God has big plans for you! And you can be confident in His plans for you because every day He is growing YOU into a courageous girl. He will be your constant companion and will give you just the strength you need to choose faith over fear.

These devotions and prayers were written with you in mind. They are lovely reminders of the power you have because you're God's girl. Touching on topics that matter to you, like family, friendships, trust, hope, and prayer, these inspiring readings will help you grow a deeper relationship with God as you also grow into the courageous girl He designed you to be.

You are not weak. With Him by your side, you can stand strong—no matter what.

The Courage to Be Yourself

"Have I not told you? Be strong and have strength of heart!
Do not be afraid or lose faith. For the Lord your
God is with you anywhere you go."
JOSHUA 1:9

Sometimes you feel so alone, like no one is on your side. You think people at school don't like you or don't want to be your friend. And you're afraid to be who God made you to be because you're sure others won't like what they see.

But just as He told Joshua, God wants you to dig deep and find the courage to be yourself. He made you on purpose, and He delights in you! Even more, He promises to never unfriend you or reject you no matter what. He loves your quirky coolness!

So, when you feel alone and are scared to let others really know who you are, remember that you are amazing. Be brave enough to push through the fear and be the true you!

God, thank You for making me. Help me love all the
quirky and cool things about who I am, and help
me have the courage to let others see them too.

The courage to wait

Wait for the Lord. Be strong.
Let your heart be strong. Yes, wait for the Lord.
PSALM 27:14

No one likes to wait. We want what we want right now. Think about it. Isn't it torture to wait to open your birthday or Christmas presents? And standing in that long line to ride the double-loopty-loop roller coaster is agony. Even waiting for your friends to show up for a sleepover can feel like too much to handle. But learning to wait for God is often harder, and it takes courage.

What are the things you've been asking God for? Maybe you need help with a friendship or a hard class at school. Maybe you're hoping to make the team or the musical, and you've been praying about it. It's easy to give up when the answer doesn't come quickly. Waiting isn't something anybody likes.

While God always answers our prayers, sometimes it takes a while to work out the details. We need to have courage to wait and trust Him.

God, would You please give me strength to wait for Your answers
to my prayers? And thanks for always hearing me when I ask.

Don't Be Afraid

"Do not be afraid. For I have bought you and made you free.
I have called you by name. You are Mine!"
ISAIAH 43:1

What are the things that scare you the most? Is it fear of monsters under your bed? Getting in trouble with your parents? Being lost? Are you afraid of heights, dogs, or losing your best friend? Fears are real, but they are not from God.

When fear starts to creep up on you, remember that God promises to never leave you alone. And because He is God and loves you so much, He will never break a promise. You may not be able to see Him with your eyes, but you can talk to Him and ask for courage. You can ask for help. And you can ask God to make you feel safe and secure. . .anytime and anywhere. He is always with you.

God, I'm glad that I am Yours! Help me stay free from fear.
I will remember to ask for Your help when I'm scared.

YOU ARE STRONG

Be strong. Be strong in heart, all you who hope in the Lord.
PSALM 31:24

If you love Jesus and have Him in your heart, you have access to His strength. Sometimes we feel weak because we're facing something that feels bigger than we are. Maybe your parents are getting divorced or you lost a grandparent. Maybe girls at school are being mean or you didn't make the team. Maybe your grades aren't as good as you'd like them to be or your doctor just gave you bad news about your health. These are the kinds of situations that can make you feel exhausted and ready to give up.

Remember that you are human, which means you have human-sized strength. But God has God-sized strength that will never run out! He has an endless supply to give to you! So, when you find yourself scared and feeling helpless, remember that because of Jesus you are strong! All you have to do is ask Him for courage to face your fears, and He will happily give you exactly what you need.

God, thank You for helping me when I feel weak.
Sometimes I just need Your help.

Fear Is Not from God

For God did not give us a spirit of fear. He gave us a spirit of power and of love and of a good mind.
2 TIMOTHY 1:7

What a good reminder for when you feel scared about something: fear *doesn't* come from God. He doesn't use fear to make you obey. Being worried or full of anxiety is never something God wants for you. So, it's important to remember that when you feel scared about anything, it is absolutely not from God.

Do you know what He did give you? Access to His power and strength and a clear mind to choose the right things and make good decisions. He packed you full of awesomeness, and He'll even share His awesomeness when you need it. The last thing God wants is for you to be afraid, worried, or stressed out. That's not His plan for someone He loves so deeply.

Keep your chin up, and ask God for what you need every day. And never forget that you are amazing!

God, thank You for giving me Your goodness. Please help me live fearlessly every day and in every way.

you will have trouble, but. . .

*"I have told you these things so you may have peace
in Me. In the world you will have much trouble.
But take hope! I have power over the world!"*

JOHN 16:33

When Jesus says He has power over the world, it means that *nothing* will ever be too big for Him to handle. It means that *nothing* is above Him or equal to Him. It means that *nothing* will catch Him off guard or be too hard to figure out. What that means for you is that Jesus has your back.

The Bible says that you will have trouble, but it's your relationship with Jesus that gives you the courage to work through it. Think about it. Where is life hard for you right now? Are you struggling with a friend or fighting with your sibling? Are you in trouble with your parents or a teacher? Jesus has a plan that will bring you peace, so be brave and ask Him for help. He will help you find the way.

*God, will You please help me? I'm in trouble
and need to fix things that are messed up.*

when people are mean

So we can say for sure, "The Lord is my Helper.
I am not afraid of anything man can do to me."
HEBREWS 13:6

Chances are you know some people who are just nasty. Maybe it's someone in your math class or on your soccer team. It could be a mean girl in your neighborhood or a rude boy in youth group. It could even be someone in your own family who is cranky and takes their bad attitude out on you. Whenever people like this get the chance, they say things and do things that make you feel unlovable, unlikable, and like you just don't fit in.

Have you ever talked to God about it? Today's verse reminds you that He is the One always willing to help you when you're in a tough place. The writer of this scripture knows it for sure and makes a courageous choice by saying he isn't afraid of the meanies. Because he is sure that God will help, he decides not to let them steal his joy. Where do you need that kind of courage?

God, help me be strong so I don't doubt
myself when others are mean.

God's Strength Gives You Courage

This is the last thing I want to say:
Be strong with the Lord's strength.
EPHESIANS 6:10

We often save the best for last, don't we? We eat our dessert last. We save the biggest present to open last. We wait until the very end to tell the punch line of a joke and share the best part of the story after all the other details. The end is usually saved for the most important.

In this letter, Paul saved a big gold nugget of truth for the end. He reminded his readers that their strength came from God. Paul himself knew that his courage to stand strong in scary times was because of the Lord, and he wanted to make sure we understood that too.

You may be strong and able to work through hard things on your own. Parents and friends might help too. But when you reach the end of your own abilities and are feeling scared or worried about how everything will turn out, ask for God's help. He'll give you supernatural courage.

God, I need Your help to figure things out.
Please give me strength.

Keep Moving Forward

"'But now be strong, Zerubbabel,' says the Lord. 'Be strong,
Joshua son of Jehozadak, head religious leader. And be strong,
all you people of the land,' says the Lord. 'Do the work,
for I am with you,' says the Lord of All."
HAGGAI 2:4

Sometimes we let our fears paralyze us. Rather than do the next right thing, we give up. Instead of trying again, we walk away. We lose our confidence and end up quitting the team, leaving the group, or ending a friendship.

It takes courage to keep moving forward when things are hard. You have to dig deep to find the grit to keep trying when you feel hopeless and helpless. But God promises to give you the power so you can do what needs to be done. He promises to be there with you all the way and to help you be fearless.

What is God asking you to do that feels big? Remember that you are strong and courageous with Him!

God, I need You to help me move forward. Thank You for
standing with me through it all and giving me what I need.

Help Others to Be Bold

Every one helps each other, and says to his brother, "Be strong!"
ISAIAH 41:6

Sometimes you need help to feel courageous, but other times it's your friends and family who need it. Did you know that God made you to need other people? He decided life would be better if you were surrounded with parents, siblings, and besties who encouraged you. That's right, you were never meant to be alone in your struggles.

Can you think of someone who always makes you feel brave? Someone who gives you the guts to stand up for yourself? Someone who loves you and makes you feel confident? They are a gift from God, and you are blessed to have them!

Now think about this. Who needs you to be their cheerleader right now? Who's in a tough place and needs a pep talk? Who needs to be reminded that God is bigger than their fear? Ask God to give them a big dose of His courage today!

God, help me see the people in my life who need me to remind them to be strong and bold. I want to help them when they need it.

courage to face tough situations

"When you pass through the waters, I will be with you.
When you pass through the rivers, they will not flow over you.
When you walk through the fire, you will not be
burned. The fire will not destroy you."
ISAIAH 43:2

It takes courage to face hard situations. Sometimes we have to put on our big-girl pants and walk right through because we know it's the only way—the *best* way—to heal. It might look like this. . .

When your friend is mad at you, you don't let the anger build up. Instead, you go right to her and apologize. When you let down your mom, rather than act like nothing happened, you do what needs to be done to make it better. When you have a tough choice to make, you find the determination to choose the right one.

It may feel like a lonely road, but you are not alone. God promises to be with you all the way to the end.

God, help me be brave when life gets hard. And thank You
for keeping me company through anything I may face.

Don't Be Afraid to Cry

You have seen how many places I have gone.
Put my tears in Your bottle. Are they not in Your book?
PSALM 56:8

There are lots of things in life that are tear worthy. You lose someone you loved, your feelings got hurt, you didn't get invited to the party, you made a bad grade, your parents got divorced. . .or a million other yucky things happen. It can feel lonely, but God sees every tear you cry. He collects them because they matter to Him.

Crying is a good, healthy way to let out our emotions. And sometimes it takes courage for us to be honest about how we feel rather than stuffing it down and acting like everything is okay. While some people may not like our tears, God welcomes them. He is always a safe place to be real with our feelings.

Who in your family lets you cry it out and hugs you until it's better? Who are the friends you can cry with? Be grateful. They are gifts from God. But never forget that He is a safe cry buddy too.

God, give me courage to be honest about my feelings.

Fight for Peace

"Peace I leave with you. My peace I give to you. I do not give
peace to you as the world gives. Do not let your
hearts be troubled or afraid."
JOHN 14:27

Sometimes it's hard to fight for peace because it seems everything around us is crazy. It's easy to let worry take over and allow the stress to set in.

Think about it. Have you ever been so nervous about a test that you couldn't sleep at night? Or have you been worried about a friend and you couldn't focus in class? Maybe you've been anxious about a game or your part in the musical and it made you sick to your stomach. Fighting for peace requires determination to reach out to God rather than try to handle it in your own strength.

When you ask Him for peace, He will give it to you, and it will be exactly what you need to calm your heart so you're not stressed out by life. Where do you need His help right now?

God, sometimes life feels so big. I know I am a worrier,
so I'm asking for Your peace to take over my life.

you can do anything. . .with Jesus

I can do all things because Christ gives me the strength.
PHILIPPIANS 4:13

What things overwhelm you? Are there things you've quit because they were just too hard? Did something look too scary to try, so you didn't? Have you ever walked away from a challenge because you felt weak and vulnerable?

It's common to look at the things life throws our way and say, "Um. . .no thanks. I'll pass." Sometimes it's just too hard. But when we let those tests and trials scare us away, we're forgetting one very important truth: you have Jesus on your side. That means with His help, you can do anything you choose to do.

What do you want to try but are too afraid? What do you need to do but don't feel equipped to do it? Is there something you are hoping to have that seems too risky to fight for? Well, guess what? You can do *all* things. . .because Jesus will give you strength if you ask.

God, I need the courage that comes from Your strength because I feel helpless right now.

courage to Hope

Our hope comes from God. May He fill you with joy and
peace because of your trust in Him. May your hope
grow stronger by the power of the Holy Spirit.
ROMANS 15:13

It takes courage to be hopeful. Can you think of times when you really hoped for something—the fight with your brother to be over, an invite to the cool-kid party, a friend to hang out with, your parents to stop arguing and get along—and it never happened? Sometimes our hope dries up because what we want the most doesn't happen.

In those times, when we come to the end of our hope, we can ask God for more. He has endless amounts and will give us an extra dose or two when we need it. He isn't too busy to help, and our requests don't ever annoy Him. So, find the courage to ask for the hope you need to stay strong and encouraged while you wait for God to make things right.

God, holding on to hope is hard, and I need You to
strengthen me as I trust Your will and timing.

GOD MAKES FEAR GO AWAY

I looked for the Lord, and He answered me.
And He took away all my fears.
PSALM 34:4

Did you notice in today's scripture that God took away *all* of the psalmist's fears? He didn't take away one or just a few. Instead, when the writer found the courage to take those fears to the Lord, God removed *every single one* of them.

Take a minute to list all the fears that are worrying you right now. Do you have doubts about your talents? Are you worried about your friendships? Are you unsure about your grades or if you'll be good enough to make the team? Maybe you're dreading a conversation that needs to happen or an upcoming appointment. Where is anxiety getting the best of you?

Today, make time to list all those fears and give them to God. Ask Him for the courage to be strong when you're scared. He promises to hear you, answer you, and put those fears in their place.

God, I am full of worry and doubt about many things in my life. Would You please help me be brave and trust You?

The Courage to Be Kind

God has chosen you. You are holy and loved by Him. Because of this, your new life should be full of loving-pity. You should be kind to others and have no pride. Be gentle and be willing to wait for others.
COLOSSIANS 3:12

Sometimes it's easy to forget that you're fully loved by God. But remember that in His great compassion, He chose you. When you asked Jesus into your heart, inviting Him to be your Savior, it changed the way you live your life.

Rather than be mean, moody, or mad, you have God's power to be compassionate toward those around you. You're to be kind and understanding to your friends and family, just as God is to you. But it takes courage because people aren't always nice back. You must have the guts to be kindhearted to others even when they are not kind to you.

What is the hardest part about loving others? Who does God want you to be kind to right now?

God, I need Your help to be kind. Help me love others, even the ones who don't treat me well.

Hard Times Lead to Great Things

The little troubles we suffer now for a short time are making us ready for the great things God is going to give us forever.
2 CORINTHIANS 4:17

Have you heard the saying "What doesn't kill you makes you stronger"? It means if you stay strong and brave in hard situations, you'll come out the other side stronger, wiser, and able to better handle the next tough circumstance.

Can you think of a time when this was true in your life? Maybe you had a bad fight with your best friend, and it taught you how to work through the next argument. Or maybe you got in trouble with your parents for talking back to them, and instead of making a snarky comment the next time, you chose to be respectful.

We have to face hard times before we can get to great times. God never tells us this life will be easy. But our suffering isn't wasted. Every difficult thing you face is training for a better future.

God, give me courage to stay strong when times are hard, because I know it will lead to something good.

who you gonna call?

You answered me on the day I called.
You gave me strength in my soul.
PSALM 138:3

Have you ever had a rotten, no-good, totally terrible day? One where someone hurt your feelings, made you angry, messed something up, or expected too much? Maybe you failed a big test, didn't make the team, got cut from the play, or were sent to the principal's office. Chances are you can remember a day like that pretty easily. And sometimes, it takes all the courage we have to just get through bad days.

When those kinds of days happen, who do you go to for help? We all have our people. For you it may be a friend, your mom, a youth leader, a teacher, or even a sibling. God gives us awesome community to help walk us through hard days. But God is ultimately where we get our strength.

The next time you have a rotten, no-good, totally terrible day, ask God to make you brave. He'll get you through it.

God, I know bad days are a part of life. Please give me
everything I need to handle them. Make me brave.

The courage to share

"For we must tell what we have seen and heard."
ACTS 4:20

Do you talk about Jesus with your friends? Do your classmates at school know that you are a Christian and that you love God? Sometimes it's scary to be bold about our faith because we're afraid of being judged or people making fun of us. Rather than be loud and proud Jesus girls, we choose to keep that part of our life a secret.

Have you ever asked God to give you the courage you need to talk about Him with others? He never intended for you to navigate hard conversations alone. Even in Bible times, people prayed to God and asked Him to make them brave so they could share their faith. It's okay to need His help. And even more, it's okay to ask for it. God is hoping you will!

You're on the earth to be a light, pointing others to Jesus. Sometimes we use words, and other times we let our actions speak instead. But either way, ask God for courage to share Him with those around you.

God, I want to share You with others!
Give me strength to live boldly.

Be Brave

"Go, gather together all the Jews who are in Susa, and have them all go without food so they can pray better for me. Do not eat or drink for three days, night or day. I and my women servants will go without food in the same way. Then I will go in to the king, which is against the law. And if I die, I die."

ESTHER 4:16

Talk about a courageous woman! Esther had important news that would save her people from death, but she knew telling her husband, the king, might mean her own death. He wasn't a warm and fuzzy leader but instead a prideful, mean, unpredictable ruler who didn't know God. Esther chose to be brave anyway.

What circumstances require your bravery right now? Where do you need to stand up for what's right but are worried about what might happen if you do? Who needs to hear the truth from you?

Make time this week to read the rest of Esther's story, because her bravery will encourage you to be brave too!

God, help me not give in to fear when I need to be gutsy.

Be Strong. Be Fearless.

Then David said to his son Solomon, "Be strong. Have strength of heart, and do it. Do not be afraid or troubled, for the Lord God, my God, is with you. He will not stop helping you. He will not leave you until all the work of the house of the Lord is finished."
1 CHRONICLES 28:20

This verse is packed with valuable gold nuggets that can be mined even today. It offers a peek into a father-son moment when David reminds his son Solomon that God is his power source for the massive job ahead of him. He needed to be reminded that God would be with him to the very end.

What in this verse from Chronicles stands out the most? What part of it encourages your heart? What words give you strength to face your situation with bravery?

Take time today to write out this verse, and personalize it by inserting your name at the beginning of each sentence. Read it out loud to yourself every time fear begins to creep in. God is with you, sweet girl. You can do it!

God, thank You for reminding me I can be strong and fearless because You are with me.

stand up to peer pressure

Then Peter and the missionaries said,
"We must obey God instead of men!"
ACTS 5:29

It's hard to stay true to what you know is right when others try to convince you to do something you know is wrong. It may be innocent, like staying awake longer at a sleepover. Or it may be something dangerous, like trying drugs. Either way, find the nerve to stand your ground and not give in.

If you ask God what He thinks about the hard choices you're facing, He'll tell you. Here are a few ways you can hear His voice:

1. Read the Bible (it's how God reveals Himself).
2. Listen to the gut feeling that warns you.
3. Pray for wisdom to know His will.

Just as Peter declared he was going to listen to and obey God rather than give in to the thoughts and suggestions of godless men, you can choose to do the same. When you do, God will bless your courage to do what's right instead of what's popular.

God, I'm listening. Help me hear You so I make wise choices.

The Courage to Give Thanks

In everything give thanks. This is what God
wants you to do because of Christ Jesus.
1 Thessalonians 5:18

When you're in a tough situation, what's your first reaction? When you and your best friend are fighting or your parents ground you, what do you do? When you're feeling rejected or your secret is shared by a friend you trusted, how do you handle it?

Chances are you get angry or sad, and you might even throw a pity party so you can feel sorry for yourself. You're not alone; every one of us does this from time to time. But what if you started giving thanks instead, just like today's verse says to do?

You could thank God that He will always love you and that He promises to never unfriend you. You could thank God for being 100 percent trustworthy and always willing to listen when you share your pain with Him. It takes courage to praise when you would rather pout. But when you do, it will change how you feel. . .every time.

God, give me strength to see the good and be thankful!

The Courage to Not Give Up

" 'For I know the plans I have for you,' says the Lord, 'plans for well-being and not for trouble, to give you a future and a hope.' "
JEREMIAH 29:11

This is why we don't give up. This powerful reminder from Jeremiah is why we stay strong when we want to crumble. This promise is the reason we find the courage to get up, wipe off the dirt, and try again when we fall. Reread the verse out loud.

God created beautiful plans for your life. He knows every detail of your future, something your parents don't even know. God's plans for you are filled with good things and hard things, and both will give you a sense of hope if you let them.

Be brave, courageous girl. Don't allow tough times to steal your joy or kill your confidence, because God is with you, walking out every single day of life with you. Anything you face has to be approved by Him, so trust that if He has allowed it, there is a very good reason for it.

God, thank You for knowing my future.
Give me the courage to walk it out.

An Invitation to Be Brave

Where can I go from Your Spirit? Or where can I run away from where You are? If I go up to heaven, You are there! If I make my bed in the place of the dead, You are there! If I take the wings of the morning or live in the farthest part of the sea, even there Your hand will lead me and Your right hand will hold me.

PSALM 139:7–10

This verse is an invitation to be brave no matter what scary and hard things you are facing right now. The writer is sharing with you a reminder that God is always with you, and there is nowhere you can hide from Him. He sees everything that scares you and knows what makes you worry. He sees every tear that falls down your cheek. He knows the thoughts that make you doubt yourself. And because God loves you so much, He promises to be close to you and never leave your side.

Simply put, no matter if you're in good times or hard times, God is there to lead you and hold you.

God, because of You I am brave. Thank You!

Have the Guts to Ask God

Those who are right with the Lord cry, and He hears them.
And He takes them from all their troubles. The Lord is near
to those who have a broken heart. And He saves
those who are broken in spirit.
PSALM 34:17–18

Do you ever think your problems are too small to bring to God? With all the mess, muck, and mire in the world today, do you think God is too busy to hear you? Maybe you've decided He only wants to hear the big problems, not the everyday hurts and frustrations you're facing right now. But know this: that couldn't be further from the truth.

God has the supernatural ability to hear from everyone at the same time and give them His full attention. He can multitask like a pro. God delights in every part of you—the good, the bad, and everything in between. He wants to hear from you. And whether it's something big or something small, it all matters to Him. Because *you* matter to Him.

God, give me the guts to ask for Your help in all things.
I love that You love me so much.

Fearless Faith

*Our life is lived by faith. We do not live by
what we see in front of us.*
2 CORINTHIANS 5:7

Sometimes it would be easier to trust God if we could see Him. If we could talk face-to-face and see His expressions, it would make God more real. Or if we could literally crawl up onto His lap and be comforted, it would strengthen our belief. It's hard not to see God, isn't it?

While you may not see His face before you go to heaven, you've most certainly seen His handiwork. Think about it. Has God fixed something you asked Him to? Did He heal someone? Did an impossible situation work out in your favor? Did you overcome fear and have a burst of courage to speak up? Did you ace the test? Did you make friends? Did you have the confidence to try something new?

All of those times are faith builders. They're reminders that you don't have to see God's face to trust Him. And when you're feeling weak or scared, just ask Him for fearless faith.

God, I don't need to see You to believe in You. I love You!

overcoming the what-ifs

*But the Lord has been my strong place, my God,
and the rock where I am safe.*

PSALM 94:22

Feeling safe and secure is a basic human need. Life can often make us nervous or fearful because it's unpredictable. No matter how hard we try to control everything, we just can't always know what tomorrow will bring, and it sometimes feels too big and scary.

Do you live in the what-ifs?

- What if I try and fail?
- What if they don't like me?
- What if I embarrass myself?
- What if I trust people and they let me down?

God uses scripture like Psalm 94:22 to remind you that He will be your safe place. With Him, the what-ifs lose their power because He promises to give you strength when you need it. Your job is to be bold enough to trust that God is for you and will help you every time you ask.

*God, I need You to smash the what-ifs that keep me from
trusting You. Help me be bold and have confidence
in You more than in what scares me.*

Are You a Drama Queen?

God is our safe place and our strength. He is always our help
when we are in trouble. So we will not be afraid, even if the
earth is shaken and the mountains fall into the center of
the sea, and even if its waters go wild with storm
and the mountains shake with its action.
PSALM 46:1–3

The psalmist is trying to calm our anxious heart and remind us that even if the worst scenario happens, God is with us. So often, we go negative in our thoughts. . . .

When you're in a fight with your friend, you're sure you two will never make up. When you fail a test, you decide you'll never pass your grade. When you disappoint your parents, you're afraid they'll never trust you again. Let's admit that sometimes we can all be drama queens. Amen?

What if you decided to be gutsy and retrain those drama-queen behaviors? Rather than take the crazy train to worst-scenario land, what if you instead prayed to God about what's bothering you? Rather than freak out, try asking for courage, strength, peace, or whatever you need.

God, remind me to ask You for help!

The Nerve to Be Strong

Be happy in your hope. Do not give up when trouble comes.
Do not let anything stop you from praying.
ROMANS 12:12

Sometimes being strong is the last thing you want to be. You'd rather hide under your covers, or eat a tub of ice cream, or binge-watch your favorite Netflix show. It takes real guts and determination to put on your big-girl pants and be brave.

Where do you need to be strong right now? Do you need to stand up for yourself or stand up for someone else? Is there a tough circumstance you have to walk through? Are you dealing with a hard family situation? Maybe you need to find the courage to fess up to something you've done.

According to Romans 12:12, you can choose to be full of hope for a good outcome. You can dig deep for the strength to not give up, and you can find the motivation to pray through it all. Today, choose to believe this, and walk it out every day.

God, will You give me the nerve to be strong
so I can face the hard times?

God Is Bigger

What can we say about all these things?
Since God is for us, who can be against us?
ROMANS 8:31

Does it ever feel like the whole world is against you? You and your friends are fighting for silly reasons. Your teacher doesn't seem to like you or want you to succeed. Your coach cut your play time in half and you're not sure why. You get in trouble with your parents for the littlest things. Your siblings are acting especially mean. And everywhere you turn, it feels like people dislike you.

Believe it or not, those kinds of feelings are normal. Life can be hard, and it can make us feel all alone. Our problems can look like giants, making us feel like ants next to them. But God is for us. And that means nothing can run us over because He will always protect us.

Yes, you will have troubles and problems. But God is bigger and will give you the courage to face anything life throws at you.

God, I'm so glad You are for me.
Please help me be confident and strong.

Filling in the Gaps

"For God can do all things."
LUKE 1:37

On your own, your strength to handle problems is limited. You can only deal with so much friend drama. There is an end to your patience with that classmate who loves to annoy you. And your sibling only gets so much grace from you before things get ugly. Yes, you have limits.

But you also have a secret weapon that's available whenever you need it. God is ready to fill in the gaps that need filling. He didn't create you to be able to handle everything on your own. He gave you parents and friends to support you. But He also promises to be there whenever you need His help.

What feels like it's too much right now? Where are you struggling to hold it together? Where can't you figure things out? Who is hard to love right now?

When you're feeling like you don't have the courage and strength to take one more step, ask God for help.

God, I can't do this on my own.
Will You please fill in the gaps for me?

Fear vs. Trust

When I am afraid, I will trust in You. I praise the Word
of God. I have put my trust in God. I will not
be afraid. What can only a man do to me?
PSALM 56:3–4

Every day you have tons of choices to make. What cute outfit will you wear? Who will you sit by at lunch? What games will you play at recess? Will you do homework or watch TV after school? But one of the most important choices you get to make is whether you will be afraid or whether you will trust God.

Just like choices, there are tons of opportunities each day to be scared. Think for a minute about what scared you today or yesterday. What made you worry? Where did you feel anxious? Did a concern keep you awake last night? Chances are you found a few fears tucked away in your day.

But there's good news! If you talk to God about those fears, you can know for sure He will help. So, when fear pops up again, you can choose to trust He is already working on it.

God, help me trust You rather than fear something else.

what matters most

*"Gather together riches in heaven where they will not be eaten
by bugs or become rusted. Men cannot break in and steal them.
For wherever your riches are, your heart will be there also."*
MATTHEW 6:20–21

Today's verse is a warning of sorts. It asks us to peek into
ourselves and consider what is the most important thing to
us. We may say it's God or church or family, but is it really?
Think about what gets the majority of your time. Instagram?
Friends? Video games or Netflix? Sports or books? Makeup
or fashion?

The hard truth is that whatever gets your attention the
very most is what you value the very most. It's hard to say no
to friends because you need to spend time reading the Bible
instead or skip the premiere of your favorite TV show because
you planned to spend time journaling your prayers to God.
But when you have the courage to invest in your relationship
with God, it makes all the difference in your day.

*God, my heart is with You. Give me the determination
I need to make You number one in my life.*

Giving up the Need to control

Be quiet and know that I am God. I will be honored
among the nations. I will be honored in the earth.
PSALM 46:10

Wanting to be in control is part of being human. Everyone, at least on some level, wants to be in control of things around them because it makes them feel safer. Can you relate?

What are the things you try to control? Maybe you are the leader of your group of friends or the captain of the team because you like to make decisions. Maybe you boss around your little brother or sister because you're certain you know better. Maybe you don't listen to suggestions because you want to choose for yourself. Where are you playing God in your life?

Today's verse is so good and true. It's a powerful reminder that God is God. . .and we are not. And since we often crave to be in control, choosing to let God lead is a very brave decision.

You can still be a leader, but let God show you the way.

God, I give You control of my life.
Give me the courage to follow You.

praying the gritty prayers

You must keep praying. Keep watching!
Be thankful always.
COLOSSIANS 4:2

Prayer is a powerful weapon when it feels like everything around you is crumbling. It keeps you focused on Jesus rather than on the struggles you're facing. When you pray, you are calling heaven down to earth, asking for God to help out in a situation. There's no doubt that prayer is one of the most effective weapons you have.

What does prayer look like in your life?

Today's verse tells us to keep praying. It's a clue for you. It's a cue to not give up in prayer. Sometimes we think that asking once is all we need. While that can be true, most of the time we need to pray whenever God brings a person or situation to mind. Why? It's not because God needs reminding. It's because it gives us courage, strength, wisdom, peace, or whatever else we need to keep going.

So, keep praying, courageous girl. God is listening.

God, give me the resolve to pray until my request is answered.

God Is Always There

The Lord said, "I Myself will go with you.
I will give you rest."
EXODUS 33:14

God is always with you. Sometimes we think He is only in church or shows up only at youth group. We decide He is with those who need Him the very most—ones who need Him more than we do. But your heavenly Father stays close to you every minute of every day.

That means in the moments you feel alone, you really aren't. God is right there with you. The times when you're facing hard decisions that are scary, God will show you the way. When you feel rejected by friends, God will comfort you. He sees every tear and knows every heartache. God sees your courage and bravery. And He chooses to be with you because He delights in who you are.

How does this truth make you feel? In what ways does it encourage and comfort you? How does it change your understanding of the relationship you have with God?

God, I'm so glad to know You are always with me. Your presence makes me feel brave, and I love You with all my heart!

You Are Beautiful Just the Way You Are

But the Lord said to Samuel, "Do not look at the way he looks on the outside or how tall he is, because I have not chosen him. For the Lord does not look at the things man looks at. A man looks at the outside of a person, but the Lord looks at the heart."

1 SAMUEL 16:7

It's very hard to be confident in how you look, especially in today's world. Feeling good about who you are isn't easy.

We see ads on TV or in magazines featuring girls we don't look like but wish we did. Instagram fills our heads with what society says is beautiful, and it makes us feel not good enough. The world's ideas of beauty set us up to feel unlovable.

But God reminds us of what's truly important—the heart. Find the courage to focus on being kind and generous and loving rather than focusing solely on what's on the outside. Yes, you are beautiful, just the way you are.

God, help me be confident in who I am.
And help me love the way You made me!

NOPE, NOTHING

For I know that nothing can keep us from the love of God.
Death cannot! Life cannot! Angels cannot! Leaders cannot!
Any other power cannot! Hard things now or in the future
cannot! The world above or the world below cannot!
Any other living thing cannot keep us away from the
love of God which is ours through Christ Jesus our Lord.
ROMANS 8:38–39

Think for a minute. What are the things you could do or the words you could speak that would cause God to turn His back on you? Think about the most trouble you've gotten into, or the snarkiest comment you've made to your mom, or the meanest thing you have done to your best friend. Do you believe any of those made God walk away?

Here's the truth. Just like today's verses say, there is nothing—*nothing*—that can keep you from God's love. You simply cannot do or say anything that will cause God to walk away from you. In a world where things change all the time, His love never does. It's rock solid.

God, help me face the truth that Your
love is forever and for always!

Putting on a Brave Face

This is the day that the Lord has made.
Let us be full of joy and be glad in it.
PSALM 118:24

Sometimes you have to put on a brave face in the world. Maybe the day before was awful, and you would rather hide in a hole than leave the comfort of your bed. Maybe life has been tough lately because your family is going through a divorce or you've lost someone to an illness. It takes real determination to go about your day when you are sad or discouraged.

But God created today, and He decided to have you be a part of it. He wanted you here. He made sure your eyes opened this morning. And even though you may be in a mess, you can choose to be full of joy anyway.

No, you don't have to be happy that life is super hard right now. That's not realistic. But you *can* choose to find joy in other places. Take a minute to name a few of those things right now.

God, I want to be joyful even when life is hard.
Will You help me do that?

peace and strength

*The peace of God is much greater than the human mind
can understand. This peace will keep your hearts
and minds through Christ Jesus.*
PHILIPPIANS 4:7

What makes you feel peaceful? Is it hanging out with your friends or curling up for family movie night? Is it a hot bath complete with bubbles and a face mask? Maybe it comes from listening to music, journaling, or reading a good book. All of these are good! Finding freedom from life's yuckies is good for our heart and our health.

But even with these good options, the best peace you can ever have is the peace you get from Jesus. Have you ever asked Him for it? He offers the kind of peace that doesn't make any sense to others, because they'd be freaking out if they were in your shoes. His peace will help you get through anything.

When you can't find courage to get through your day. . . when you don't feel strong enough. . .when you're scared—pray for God to fill you with His peace.

God, would You bring peace and comfort to me right now?

The courage to step out

Jesus said, "Come!" Peter got out of the boat and walked on the water to Jesus. But when he saw the strong wind, he was afraid. He began to go down in the water. He cried out, "Lord, save me!"
MATTHEW 14:29–30

Can you imagine the courage it took for Peter to leave the safety of the boat and step out onto the water where gravity would pull him down? You may not have been asked to do what Jesus asked of Peter, but can you remember a time it took every bit of courage to do something hard or scary?

Where is God asking you to be brave right now? What scares you the very most about it? What keeps you from trusting God enough to step out and do the next right thing?

When you need a big dose of courage, God is the One who will give you the exact amount you need. You may try to figure it out on your own, you may pledge to be gutsy. . .but your bravery will never match His. And luckily, it doesn't have to.

God, I want to live fearlessly. Please help me be brave!

Dare to Rest

"Come to Me, all of you who work and have heavy loads. I will give you rest. Follow My teachings and learn from Me. I am gentle and do not have pride. You will have rest for your souls. For My way of carrying a load is easy and My load is not heavy."
MATTHEW 11:28–30

These days, our schedules are crazy. Between school, after-school stuff, youth group, and homework, we can barely find time to rest. We are so overscheduled and super overcommitted, and it leaves us exhausted. And while it leaves us physically tired, it also makes us tired emotionally. It takes a lot of mental energy to be so busy!

So, what do you do when you're worn out?

God invites you to take every bit of your exhaustion and give it to Him. He will restore your soul if you talk to Him about what's draining your energy. Ask God to give you much-needed rest today.

God, give me boldness to share with You the things that are wearing me out and draining my joy. Thank You for giving me rest in return.

Do you Have the Guts to wait?

I wait for the Lord. My soul waits and I hope in His Word.
PSALM 130:5

Waiting for God's answers is a gutsy choice because waiting is definitely one of the hardest things to do! We live in a "microwave society." We're used to getting what we want quickly.

Think about it. Have you been annoyed by a fast-food restaurant line moving too slowly? Or frustrated because the teacher didn't grade your test quickly? Maybe your parents didn't give you an answer about a party right when you wanted it or your friend didn't text you back within seconds, and it annoyed you.

When you wait for the Lord, it helps build your faith. And because waiting is and will always be a part of life, learning to wait well will bless you and grow your trust in God. He sees you. He knows the answers you need. And courageous girl, He is working on your behalf. So, find the grit to wait for God to show you the next right step.

God, please give me peace and confidence that You're working everything out for my good.

ASK IN BOLDNESS

*And my God will give you everything you need because
of His great riches in Christ Jesus.*
PHILIPPIANS 4:19

Paul reminds us in this verse that God will make sure we have
every single thing we need to survive and thrive in this life.
Here's where that gets tricky. So often what you *think* you
need and what God *knows* you need are two different things.

You may decide that unless you make the team or make
first chair in the band, you'll die. Or unless you get an invite to
a certain birthday party, you just can't go on living. Of course,
not literally, but you get the point.

The truth is that God loves you too much to give you
what you want when He knows what you really need. Your
job is to ask in boldness and then trust His answer. So, ask
away! And remember, God will always respond in ways that
are best for you!

*God, You know the desires of my heart. You know what I am
hoping for. Today I'm fearless asking for them, and I am
determined to trust Your answer no matter what.*

don't Be a worrywart

Do not worry. Learn to pray about everything.
Give thanks to God as you ask Him for what you need.
PHILIPPIANS 4:6

Take a moment and think of all the situations and people that cause you to worry. Maybe your grades are not what's expected of you. Maybe your parents have been fighting more than usual. Maybe a grandparent's health is starting to go downhill. Maybe tryouts are right around the corner. Maybe it's something completely out of your control.

God included this verse in the Bible because He knew you'd have a million reasons to worry. It's hard to live with confidence when we're so full of anxiety. Sometimes it seems like stress will never go away.

Prayer is an awesome way to get what's bothering you off your chest. God wants to hear from you, and He is available twenty-four hours a day, seven days a week. You can literally talk to Him at any time about anything. It may take some getting used to, but practice praying. It's a powerful habit to have!

God, help me stand up to worry by praying.
Thank You for always being available to me!

A supernatural transfer

The Lord God is my strength. He has made my feet like the feet of a deer, and He makes me walk on high places.
HABAKKUK 3:19

Have you ever seen a deer run in a field or dart up a hillside? They're sure-footed, which means they make it look effortless. Rather than be scared or nervous, they move with confidence because they know their bodies can do what is needed.

When you ask God to help you, you can have that same confidence because He promises to give you strength for what you're struggling with. You can access God's power to be bold and brave. It's a supernatural transfer from Him to you that gives you the guts to take the next step.

Where do you need God's strength right now? What are you facing that feels scary? Where do you need to find the courage to stand up for what's right? Spend time today talking to God about those places, and ask Him to help you be strong.

God, I know You will give me Your strength to face the hard times. Would You transfer it to me right now?

The Whole Enchilada

"You will look for Me and find Me, when you look for Me with all your heart."

JEREMIAH 29:13

Sometimes we look for the shortcut or the easy way out. We want to do the least amount of work and get the very best results. We do the bare minimum and hope for an epic outcome. And while we may be halfhearted in some areas, God wants us to be wholehearted with Him.

What does that mean for you? It means He wants you to have a deep longing to be in a relationship with Him. Rather than just hearing from you at church on Sunday or in youth group, God wants to hear from you every day. He wants the whole enchilada not just a bite.

Think about your bestie. You hang out at school, text and talk on the phone, and have tons of sleepovers. You share clothes and secrets and even finish each other's sentences. You want to be together all the time.

God wants you to have that same desire to be with Him. Choose to have an unwavering relationship with the One who created you!

God, I want You!

God is Smarter

"For as the heavens are higher than the earth, so are My ways higher than your ways, and My thoughts than your thoughts."

ISAIAH 55:9

You may be a straight-A student and on the honor roll. You may have scored the highest grade on a test or won the spelling bee. Maybe you're in advanced classes or you've been told you have wisdom beyond your years. Those are all huge accomplishments. Be proud of yourself! But God is still smarter, and that's a good thing.

God reminds us that He has endless knowledge and understanding about everything. While we only see part of the picture, He sees it from every angle. He knows why things happen and He knows how they'll turn out. He knows every single detail of your life—the good, the bad, and everything in between.

Because His ways and thoughts are higher than yours, choose to bravely trust Him. God has a hope and a future planned out for you, and while it may be bumpy at times, it will be good.

God, thank You for being smarter than I am!
Help me trust You instead of trying to figure it out myself.

Bold Declarations

But I am like a green olive tree in the house of God.
I trust in the loving-kindness of God forever and ever.
PSALM 52:8

What a bold declaration the psalmist makes here. He's putting on paper—for all to read—that he chooses to trust God's love for him, no matter what. That means all eyes will be watching to see if his statement stands up when struggles try to bring him down.

Could you make the same kind of declaration, knowing people may hold you to it?

Part of walking out your faith is being willing to stand up for it. It's being courageous and admitting that you're a Jesus girl. It's being strong even when others make fun of you for believing in God. It's not being afraid to pray in public or talk to your friends about Him.

If you ask, God will make you gutsy enough to be unashamed of your faith. It may be scary, but He will help you be fearless as you are honest about what He means in your life.

God, I want to be bold and confident in my faith
and live it out loud! Give me courage!

Live untangled

Trust in the Lord with all your heart, and do not trust in your own understanding. Agree with Him in all your ways, and He will make your paths straight.

PROVERBS 3:5–6

It's so easy for life to get all tangled up, isn't it? You may start out on the straight and narrow—following rules, being kind, minding your own business, not letting others make you mad, doing your homework and chores—but sometimes it takes just one bad choice to mess it all up.

What do you do when life gets tangled? Do you talk to a friend or a parent? Maybe you drown your frustration in video games or in homemade cookies. Maybe you journal or listen to music. We all have ways to get through life's messes. But do you ever talk to God about it?

Why not ask God what He thinks about your tangles? Ask Him to help you see things like He does. Ask for courage to take the next right step. Then tell God you're going to trust He is working out the tangles in your favor.

God, would You please straighten out my tangles?

Dare to See the Good

My Christian brothers, you should be happy when you have all kinds of tests. You know these prove your faith. It helps you not to give up.
JAMES 1:2–3

This is hard! James isn't suggesting we be happy when difficult things come into our life; he is telling us we *need* to be. He is saying we should put on our big-girl pants and be brave—brave enough to trust that God is working in the mess. James is asking us to be fearless because it's an opportunity to strengthen our faith.

How do you feel about that? How does James's statement that you should be happy in the hard stuff challenge you today?

The truth is that God is 100 percent in control and knows exactly what you need. Even more, He only allows the yuckies because He'll use them for your benefit. The hard times will make you stronger, more compassionate, wiser, and braver. While we may not like being hurt, we can choose to be happy that on the other side of it will be something good.

God, give me the courage to get through the mess with a positive attitude.

Godly Beauty

*Your beauty should come from the inside. It should come from
the heart. This is the kind that lasts. Your beauty should be
a gentle and quiet spirit. In God's sight this is of great
worth and no amount of money can buy it.*

1 PETER 3:4

Beauty has been distorted by the world. The way we decide
if someone is beautiful is often very different from how God
does.

Think about ways you and your friends define beauty. Is
it because of a girl's weight or the clothes she wears? Is it
based on how long her hair is, its color, or how she styles it?
Is someone pretty because of how she does her makeup? It's
easy to look on the outside, isn't it?

But God says beauty comes from inside because it doesn't
change with time or trends. Can you think of someone who
is kind and compassionate? A girl who treats others well and
makes smart choices? That's godly beauty, and *that* takes confidence and courage.

God, I want to be beautiful by Your definition!

supergirl strength

He answered me, "I am all you need. I give you My loving-favor.
My power works best in weak people." I am happy to be weak
and have troubles so I can have Christ's power in me.

2 CORINTHIANS 12:9

It doesn't feel good to fail at things, does it? No one likes to
think they can't do something. When it gets hard, you want
to raise your fist in the air and shout, "Girl power!" like a true
superhero. But the truth is that because you are human, you
don't have superpowers.

You do, however, have access to God's supernatural
power. That means that when you don't have the strength or
courage to take the next step, He will give you His. When you
are too afraid to act, God's power will make you brave. When
you need to do something that feels impossible, He will give
you confidence.

God, I cannot do the hard things without You.
I need Your awesome power right now!

Bravely Step Aside

Yet I am always with You. You hold me by my right hand.
You will lead me by telling me what I should do.
And after this, You will bring me into shining-greatness.
Psalm 73:23–24

Did you catch the words *and after this* in today's scripture? It's a reminder that something will happen first. It means that before the awesome thing comes, a hard or challenging thing must happen. And this passage of scripture lets us know that the requirement for the good thing was choosing to give up control and let God lead instead.

If you were to be honest, you'd probably admit that you like being in control. Who doesn't, right? When we are the ones making decisions, life feels easier. Better. It's nice to be the leader. But God wants to make sure you find the way to the shining-greatness.

He is trustworthy and wants the very best for you! And if you bravely step aside and ask God to lead your life, He will help you create something beautiful.

God, I admit I like to be in control.
But I want what You have for me even more.

An Attitude of Gratitude

Let us give thanks all the time to God through Jesus Christ.
Our gift to Him is to give thanks. Our lips should
always give thanks to His name.
HEBREWS 13:15

Talk about manners! The writer here in Hebrews wants to make sure we know the importance of giving thanks to God. Within this twenty-nine-word scripture, he tells us three times to be thankful. And since God chose to include this verse in the Bible, it must really matter that we're grateful to Him. Even more, we're told to thank Him all the time because our praise is a gift.

It's easy to ask the Lord for all the things we want, but so often we forget to thank Him for what we have. We don't tell Him how happy we are for answered prayer.

Today, write down all the things God has done for you. Then spend time in prayer, thanking Him for those things. Be bold in your thankfulness, and tell God how He helped so much. Create an attitude of gratitude to God every day.

God, You're so good to me! Thank You, thank You, thank You!

The Bad News Dare

He will not be afraid of bad news.
His heart is strong because he trusts in the Lord.
PSALM 112:7

Bad news is scary, that's for sure. From failing a test to discovering a friend's betrayal to learning your family is moving to another state, no one likes it when difficult news shows up. So how do you respond to it?

Some people get angry and throw a fit. Some cry themselves to sleep, become very sad, or bury their worries in a tub of ice cream. Others ignore it, avoid it, or refuse to believe it. But do you ever choose to trust God instead? What would that even look like?

Here is your bad-news dare. The next time something yucky happens, rather than freak out, tell God you trust Him. When sad news hits, ask God to make you courageous. Ask Him to calm your fearful heart and racing mind with His peace. Yes, there are a million reasons to be afraid of bad news, but with the Lord you don't have to be.

God, I am choosing to trust in You rather than be afraid.

Being Known

O Lord, You have looked through me and have known me.
You know when I sit down and when I get up. You understand
my thoughts from far away. You look over my path and my lying
down. You know all my ways very well. Even before
I speak a word, O Lord, You know it all.
PSALM 139:1–4

As girls, there is something wonderful about being known. Think about it. When friends surprise you with your favorite candy, or grandparents give you gift cards to stores you love the most, or Mom makes your favorite meal to celebrate your birthday, you feel important. How awesome for others to know the things that delight your heart! How amazing to be known. And how courageous to open yourself up enough for others to see the real you!

God knows you better than anyone ever could. He knows you better than you know yourself! Reread today's verses out loud, and then thank Him for caring about you so much. And ask for the confidence to continue sharing yourself with others. You are worthy of knowing!

God, thank You for creating me!
And thank You that I am known!

She Will Not Be Moved

God is in the center of her. She will not be moved.
God will help her when the morning comes.
PSALM 46:5

This verse is talking about Jerusalem and how nothing could take it down because it was a holy city. Just like that city, you too are holy if you believe in Jesus, ask Him to be the Savior of your life, and call on His name. Let's personalize this verse, because it's a powerful reminder of the truth we live out every day as Jesus girls.

Every time you see the word *her* or *she* in today's scripture, replace it with your name. Speak this out loud a few times and declare it about your life.

Then on those days when you feel rejected or betrayed, when you feel like you're unlovable or not good enough, when you're worried that everything is going to crumble around you, read that verse out loud again with your name. God will not let you be taken down. Place your courage and confidence in Him.

God, You are in the center of me.
With Your strength, I am a fighter!

Determined to Reflect Him

Then God said, "Let Us make man like Us and let him be head over the fish of the sea, and over the birds of the air, and over the cattle, and over all the earth, and over every thing that moves on the ground." And God made man in His own likeness. In the likeness of God He made him. He made both male and female.
GENESIS 1:26–27

You are made in the likeness of God. That doesn't mean you have His powers. You don't look like God since He has no body. But being made in His image means we have the ability to reflect His character in how we love others.

Are you kind and full of patience for your friends and family? Are you quick to forgive and move on? Are you loyal and loving? When you are these things for the people around you, you're reflecting His image. Yes, it can be a huge challenge to be like Him when you are tired, hungry, hurt, sad, or angry. But you can choose to be anyway.

God, I'm determined to be more like You every day.
Help me choose to reflect You to others.

Rewrite the Bully Thoughts

We break down every thought and proud thing that puts itself up against the wisdom of God. We take hold of every thought and make it obey Christ.

2 CORINTHIANS 10:5

What are the mean things you think about yourself? Do you think you're too short, too freckly, or not thin enough? Have you decided you lack talent or smarts? Maybe you bully yourself with other unkind thoughts.

Paul's advice in 2 Corinthians is awesome! He's challenging you to take those bad thoughts to God and ask His opinion. God loves every bit of your awesomeness. And while you may struggle to embrace it, He doesn't.

The next time you bully yourself with a mean thought, write it down. Think about when you started to believe it. How and why does that thought exist? Then ask God to tell you what He thinks. Write His thoughts next to your own, and then thank Him for the truth. When you do this, you're taking hold of those bully words and replacing them with God's.

God, help me stand up to the bully thoughts and rewrite them. I want to see me the way You do.

Mind Games

Peace comes when you trust God. That may sound easy, but you know giving up control is so hard because it means you don't know how it will all turn out. And honestly, that's kind of scary.

Can you think of a situation you're in right now where you feel restless and fearful? Maybe you're not sleeping well at night or you're cranky with your parents because it feels so heavy. Is it a struggle with a friend or with grades? Something at home or with a teammate? Maybe you're wrestling to make the right choice when the wrong choice feels easier. Regardless, your mind is anything but calm.

Ask God for peace. Spend time in prayer sharing with God what's worrying you. He'll make peace available to you at any moment and in any situation. He'll make those mind games settle down so your heart can rest.

*God, give me the confidence in You to ask for Your peace rather
than try to control everything. Help me trust
You more than I trust myself.*

Is That a Tomorrow Worry?

"Do not worry about tomorrow. Tomorrow will have its own worries. The troubles we have in a day are enough for one day."
MATTHEW 6:34

What are you worried about right now? Is it a test at school or an art project that's due soon? Do you have a solo in the choir program, or is your team playing in the championship? Are you moving to a new town or about to have a hard conversation with your parents? There is no shortage of worry opportunities, is there? Sometimes we carry weeks of worry on our shoulders and eventually break down in tears because it's just too much.

But God tells us to stay in today's concerns. It's hard to do, but it will help keep fear from overwhelming you. When a tomorrow worry pops into your mind, boldly say out loud, "That's not for today, so go away." Being proactive like that protects your heart and mind and keeps you focused on the things that need your attention today.

God, give me only enough strength to carry today's worries. And remind me to keep tomorrow's worries for tomorrow.

sending in the troops

For He will tell His angels to care for you and keep you in all
your ways. They will hold you up in their hands.
So your foot will not hit against a stone.
PSALM 91:11–12

Do you and your friends stick together when a messy situation comes along? Maybe the mean girl was extra mean to you today, or you found out someone was gossiping about you, and without even asking, your friends showed up to help. They protected your heart from more hurt. They told you truth to combat upsetting lies. They made sure you had support and care as they walked through the messy mess with you. Girlfriends are the best, right?

God has your back too. Without asking, He sends in His heavenly troops on your behalf. His angels have been given assignments to care and keep you. They're a line of protection to keep you safe, and they have saved you from things in life you may never even know about.

Rest assured, you are surrounded by earthly and heavenly support every day.

God, thank You! I can have confidence to take the
next right step in any situation I face.

Hard Work and God's Help

With Your help I can go against many soldiers.
With my God I can jump over a wall.
PSALM 18:29

Chances are you'll never have to fight alone against an army or jump over a towering wall. In today's verse, the psalmist is making a powerful point we don't want to miss.

Think about a situation in your life that feels too big. Is it something at school or at home? Maybe something with your own health or a huge family problem? Find something that feels so overwhelming it would take superhuman strength to get through it. It's circumstances like that where we'll only survive with God's help.

He didn't create you to go it alone. Instead, He knew all along that you'd face huge struggles that required more than you had in you. And God also planned all along to be the One to give you the courage and confidence you would need to get through them. Courageous girl, there is nothing you cannot do with hard work and God's help.

God, help me be brave enough to ask for Your help.
Thanks for always being there for me!

you get to choose

Do not act like the sinful people of the world. Let God change your life. First of all, let Him give you a new mind. Then you will know what God wants you to do. And the things you do will be good and pleasing and perfect.
ROMANS 12:2

You were created to stand out from everyone else. In all the world—past, present, and future—there will be no one else just like you. God thought you up, every detail. He chose your body type and your skin and hair color. He decided when you'd enter the world and handpicked gifts and talents just for you. To top it off, God gave you a wonderful mind and the ability to think for yourself.

That means you don't have to follow the crowd. You don't have to think and act like others. Instead, you can be courageous and make the right choices and the hard decisions that glorify God. You have the ability to be strong-minded! Be who God made you to be!

God, renew my mind so I can think for myself and make the best choices in life!

The Reason You Don't Give Up

This is the reason we do not give up. Our human body is wearing out. But our spirits are getting stronger every day.
2 CORINTHIANS 4:16

Wanting to give up is part of being human. When things get really hard, it's normal to want to quit. We lose heart because we get tired of our situation. Don't feel you're bad or wrong when these feelings come, but instead decide that today's pain and frustration won't win.

When you feel weakest is when God's strength in you is the brightest! You can ask Him for tools to keep the faith alive and to help you stay focused. Know this: You don't have to give in to peer pressure. You don't have to walk away from friendships that are tough. You don't have to give up on your dreams. You don't have to do what everyone else does just to fit in. When those moments of weakness come, all you have to do is choose to stand strong and ask God for help.

God, strengthen me! I need You to fill me with boldness so I can get through whatever comes my way.

It All Works Together

We know that God makes all things work together for the good of those who love Him and are chosen to be a part of His plan.
ROMANS 8:28

What a great truth. Somehow, in God's awesomeness, He takes everything you're dealing with and makes it good. That means all the hurt and pain. . .all the sadness and tears. . .all the frustration and anger—they're not wasted. He takes them all and creates something wonderful—something that benefits you.

Maybe you and your bestie had a bad fight, and when you finally worked it out, your friendship got stronger. Maybe your parents grounded you, and spending time at home made you realize how much you enjoyed hanging out with them. Or maybe you got a bad grade on a test, making you work even harder, and you ended up with an awesome grade in the class!

Next time something hard happens, fearlessly trust that God is working on your behalf to make something beautiful out of it. As a matter of fact, thank Him in advance!

God, I choose to trust that You will make good from the bad and happy from the sad!

who gets the credit?

*It is God Who covers me with strength
and makes my way perfect.*
PSALM 18:32

Sometimes we think we're all that, taking credit when things go right. We decide we are the reason the team won or the problem was solved. Other times we give the rock-star celebrity status to someone else, sure they're why things worked out. But the truth is that God is the One who we should be thanking.

While liking yourself and knowing your talents and skills is good and important, it's also valuable to remember that your courage, strength, and smarts come from God. Whether you realize it or not, He plays a role in your everyday life, helping you out when you need it. God covers you and directs you.

Take time today thanking God for the ways He has helped you. Ask Him for the eyes to see Him working in your life. And the next time you're able to be brave, brilliant, or bold, let God know you're thankful for Him!

*God, I give You the credit!
Thank You for helping me live the right life!*

We All Need Help

"See, God saves me. I will trust and not be afraid.
For the Lord God is my strength and song.
And He has become the One Who saves me."
ISAIAH 12:2

Can you think of a situation in your life right now where you need God's help? Something that worries you and stresses you out. Something that keeps you awake at night and is all you can think about during the day.

It could be a sick parent or grandparent, or a family member who is making bad choices. It may be teammates who aren't getting along, and you're caught in the middle trying to fix it. It could even be a nasty rumor going around school about you that is hurtful and untrue. We all have those situations that feel too big.

Why not talk to God about them? He is trustworthy and faithful, and He promises to save you when things are overwhelming and life feels out of control. Your job is to trust Him and ask for what you need.

God, I cannot do this by myself anymore. Will You give me
the courage and strength to do what needs to be done?

Choosing the Right Thing

Jesus said to her, "Martha, Martha, you are worried and troubled about many things. Only a few things are important, even just one. Mary has chosen the good thing. It will not be taken away from her."
LUKE 10:41–42

Martha and Mary were sisters. When Jesus came to their house for a visit, Martha got frustrated that her younger sister sat with the Lord rather than help in the kitchen. She was so angry, in fact, that she went to Jesus and complained, asking Him to tell Mary she needed to get back to work. Today's verse is His response to Martha's request.

What would you have done if Jesus was sitting in your house? Would you have wanted to make pizza rolls in the kitchen or sit with Him as He talked? Every day you get to choose if you spend time with God or if you don't. There are tons of other things that demand our attention. Are you determined enough to choose the right thing?

God, I want to make time for You every day.
Give me the strength to choose You over other things.

God Knows What's Best

*Be happy in the Lord. And He will give you
the desires of your heart.*
PSALM 37:4

This can be a tricky verse to understand. Some may think it means that whatever you want—cool clothes, a new iPhone, popularity—will be given to you because God wants you happy. Wouldn't that be awesome if it was that easy?

Instead, this verse is saying God will give you the desires of your heart *if* they align with His will for you. And if you are happy in the Lord, it's because you choose to trust His plan for your life. He knows what you want, and at the same time He knows what is best for you. Sometimes those two line up, and sometimes they don't. But regardless, you can be happy because you know God will take care of you either way.

Walking this out takes courage because it's choosing to be okay with God's plan even if it goes against what you really want. Sometimes it's hard to give up what you think is best.

*God, help me be happy in You! And help me trust
that Your way is the best way for me.*

Jesus Is the One

*Let us keep looking to Jesus. Our faith comes from Him and He is the
One Who makes it perfect. He did not give up when He had to suffer
shame and die on a cross. He knew of the joy that would be
His later. Now He is sitting at the right side of God.*

HEBREWS 12:2

The only One who can truly strengthen your faith is Jesus.
Of course, there are some pretty awesome people and places
that help point you to Him, like friends, youth group, church,
and family. There are also circumstances you have to face that
force you to hold on to Jesus. No doubt, God gives you many
opportunities to grow your faith and relationship in Jesus.

But we get into trouble when we let anyone or anything
take the place of Jesus. Your bestie is the bestest, but she is not
better than Jesus. Your mom is magnificent, but she can't out-
magnify Him. And youth group is great, but Jesus is greater.

Be grateful for those gifts, but let God give you strength
and courage.

God, You are my everything! Grow my faith to perfection!

He Holds Your Hand

*"For I am the Lord your God Who holds your right hand,
and Who says to you, 'Do not be afraid. I will help you.'"*
ISAIAH 41:13

God is right here with you, right now. You may not be able to see Him with your eyes or feel Him holding your hand, but chances are you can remember ways He's been there for you.

Think back over the past week. Where have you seen God move? Did He restore a friendship or give you supernatural memory during a test? Did He give you a big dose of hope when things looked hopeless? Did God comfort you in your sadness or give you courage to take the next step? God promises to help whenever you need it.

When you start to feel afraid or overwhelmed, stop and pray for His help. Don't let time pass, because that's when worry starts to pile up. He is ready and waiting to take your hand and lead you to the answers you need.

God, I know You've been working in my life even though I can't see Your face or feel Your touch. Help me live fearlessly, trusting You!

fear from the unexpected

The angel said to the women, "Do not be afraid. I know you are looking for Jesus Who was nailed to the cross. He is not here! He has risen from the dead as He said He would. Come and see the place where the Lord lay. Run fast and tell His followers that He is risen from the dead. He is going before you to the country of Galilee. You will see Him there as I have told you."
MATTHEW 28:5–7

Maybe you can relate to the woman in today's scripture. She expected one thing, but something totally different happened instead. And in that confusing moment, she was scared!

Can you relate to her instant fear? The unexpected can be scary because we're not sure what to do next. Like when you thought you rocked the test, but the failing grade is staring back at you. Or when you find a seat next to your friend at lunch, and she ignores you. We get confused, and that confusion turns to fear. But fear is never from God. And He will replace it with courage.

God, help me be brave when the unexpected hits.

oh yes, you are loved!

"The Lord your God is with you, a Powerful One Who wins the battle. He will have much joy over you. With His love He will give you new life. He will have joy over you with loud singing."
ZEPHANIAH 3:17

Ever feel unloved, like you're just a piece of trash blowing in the wind? The truth is that every day, plenty of things happen to make you feel worthless. Maybe your friend got mad at you, your parents are disappointed in you, or your coach is frustrated at your performance. So, what do you do when it seems like everyone dislikes you?

Try asking God what He thinks. He sees the truth about you and knows how amazing you are because He thought you up. Even more, God so delights in you that He literally sings over you! Even with your mess-ups, you bring Him great joy! And there is nothing you can do to make God love you any more or less than He does right now. Oh yes, courageous girl. You are very loved, indeed.

God, thank You for loving me so much!
I'm glad nothing I do will change that!

"Even If" Kind of Faith

*Even if the fig tree does not grow figs and there is no fruit on
the vines, even if the olives do not grow and the fields give no food,
even if there are no sheep within the fence and no cattle in
the cattle-building, yet I will have joy in the Lord.
I will be glad in the God Who saves me.*

HABAKKUK 3:17–18

This is a beautiful truth. The author of these verses is showing
what fearless faith looks like. No matter what's happened, the
writer knows God is still good. He knows God is still able.
And that's the kind of faith we all need.

"Even if" kind of faith says no matter the yucky and
hard circumstances you're facing today, you can still have joy
because of Jesus. Your family could be having a tough time,
your best friends may turn against you, or you could've been
cut from the school play. . .but these things don't take away
your ability to smile. Why? Because your joy comes from God
rather than from anything the world offers.

God, give me the grit I need to have "even if" kind of faith!

No Drama Llama

Let the peace of Christ have power over your hearts.
You were chosen as a part of His body. Always be thankful.
COLOSSIANS 3:15

Would your family and friends say you're a drama llama? If they were to be completely honest, do you think they'd say you tend to overexaggerate your feelings? Or would they say you're pretty steady no matter what comes your way?

Some of us are naturally a bit more dramatic in how we respond to life's heartaches and fears, but let's not forget that we also have the gift of choice. We can choose to overreact, or we can choose to take a deep breath and stay calm. No matter our usual, our responses can change if we ask God for help. When we do, He can tame the drama-llamaness so we can live with a peaceful heart.

So, the next time you get scared or hurt. . .the next time you fail or give up. . .the next time you want to freak out—be bold enough to ask for the peace of Christ instead.

God, thank You that Your peace is available
to me whenever and wherever!

every single one

Give all your worries to Him because He cares for you.
1 PETER 5:7

Reread today's verse out loud. Just how many of your worries does God want you to give to Him? One a day? Ten a week? Just the important ones? No, courageous girl. God wants every single one of your worries. The big, the small, and everything in between.

Why? Because He loves you so much and He knows life gets hard, scary, and overwhelming. He didn't create you to carry everything alone. You simply aren't that strong or powerful. In His unstoppable love for you, He chose to be available and willing to help you carry those things that feel too big and too hard.

Take a minute to let all your worries come to mind right now. For each one, tell God your fears surrounding each worry and then imagine handing them over to Him. See yourself holding the worry and then watch what happens as you place it in His hands.

God, I give You all my worries because I cannot hold them anymore. Thank You for taking them from me!

Are you asking?

*"Until now you have not asked for anything in My name.
Ask and you will receive. Then your joy will be full."*
JOHN 16:24

As Jesus girls, we're invited to ask God for what we need. Sometimes we think it's silly to ask for the small stuff, but God doesn't. We may think He is too busy to find time to listen as we ask for help with an upcoming test or frustrating friendships. We may think sharing concerns about our health or our family or even the upcoming tryouts is wasting His time. But that is absolutely not how God feels.

What keeps you from asking Him for help? You are free to ask for anything you need. God wants to have a relationship with you. And just like you have the freedom to ask your friends, your parents, your teachers, or your youth leaders for the things you need, you have that same open-door policy with God.

*God, help me be bold enough to ask You for help.
Remind me that You are able and willing
to meet every need I have.*

The Boldness of Prayer

Never stop praying.
1 Thessalonians 5:17

The Bible tells us to pray about everything. But what is prayer, and how do we do it?

Prayer is how you talk to your heavenly Father. You can talk out loud to Him, or you can pray silently. You can have long or short prayers. They don't have to sound proper or intelligent. You can even pray using bad grammar or run-on sentences.

There isn't a right time or a wrong time to pray. There's no limit on the number of prayers you can send God's way or the things you can pray about. You don't have to follow rules or guidelines. And yes, you can be bold in what you ask God to do. He wants to hear it all. You can pray directly to God anywhere, at any time, about anything.

So, whether it's about something that scares you or someone who's hurt you. . .pray. If it's excitement over getting the lead in a play. . .pray. If you need to share a secret or vent in anger. . .pray. God is always listening.

God, give me confidence to talk to You about everything!

The Power of Praying for Others

I pray that because of the riches of His shining-greatness, He will make you strong with power in your hearts through the Holy Spirit. I pray that Christ may live in your hearts by faith. I pray that you will be filled with love. I pray that you will be able to understand how wide and how long and how high and how deep His love is. I pray that you will know the love of Christ. His love goes beyond anything we can understand. I pray that you will be filled with God Himself.

EPHESIANS 3:16–19

In today's passage of scripture, Paul is praying for the church in Ephesus. He knows it's one of the kindest things he can do for the people there, because God listens when we pray.

Do you pray for others? Think of someone who is having a hard time right now. Reread Ephesians 3:16–19, this time using the person's name every time you see the words *you* and *your*. Pray this for anyone God brings to mind. It's how we love others well.

God, help me be bold enough to pray for others.

The Secret Things of God

*"The secret things belong to the Lord our God. But the things
that are made known belong to us and to our children
forever, so we may obey all the words of this Law."*
DEUTERONOMY 29:29

When bad things happen, one of the first questions we ask is
why. *Why* did this happen to me? *Why* did this happen again?
Why can't I catch a break? *Why* doesn't God protect me? *Why*
can't I get it right? *Why* are they so mean?

What *why* questions do you ask when bad happens in
your life?

While it's normal to want answers, the truth is we don't
always get to know them here on earth. Actually, we may
never understand why we're called to be brave when certain
things happen. We have to trust that the things God chooses
to keep secret are for a good reason, and if we needed to
know the *why*, we would.

The next time *why* questions flood your mind, find courage to let them know you trust God and His decision to keep
certain things secret.

God, help me keep my why questions from making me doubt You!

which way do we go?

I will show you and teach you in the way you should go.
I will tell you what to do with My eye upon you.

PSALM 32:8

With all the choices you'll need to make today, sometimes it's hard to know the right thing to do. It's confusing to make decisions when you're not sure what's best. When you're struggling to choose, who do you ask for help? Who is the person you listen to the most?

We all need friends and family to share their ideas, suggestions, and thoughts when we're looking for answers. They are a gift from God because they love us enough to help us figure out life. But if you aren't asking God for His help, you're missing out.

Your heavenly Father promises to give you direction and show you the next right step to take. Even more, He'll give you the courage you need to make decisions without fear. And He will give you confidence to know you are being smart with your choices.

God, teach me and show me what's best for me. I trust You!

Haters Gonna Hate

"Do not say what is wrong in other people's lives. Then other people will not say what is wrong in your life. Do not say someone is guilty. Then other people will not say you are guilty. Forgive other people and other people will forgive you."
LUKE 6:37

Luke 6:37 gives the perfect reason why we should not be haters. It can be hard, because girls are sometimes gossipy and judgy, but that doesn't mean you have to be. And when you are rude about others or talk behind someone's back, it sets you up for the same to happen to you.

But that reality is true on the other side as well. You see, kindness breeds kindness. Be nice to others and they will be nice to you. Forgive others and you'll be forgiven by them too. Love those around you and you will be loved right back.

Don't judge people. Don't be critical. Instead, find the guts and grit to be different. Haters gonna hate, but you can love.

God, I don't want to be mean and rude. I know everyone is battling something. Help me be a force for good in the world.

put on jesus

I will have much joy in the Lord. My soul will have joy in my God,
for He has clothed me with the clothes of His saving power. He has
put around me a coat of what is right and good, as a man at his own
wedding wears something special on his head, and as a bride
makes herself beautiful with stones of great worth.

ISAIAH 61:10

Every day, you get to choose whether you put on Jesus. You can walk out the door full of love and kindness, or you can walk out with bitterness and unforgiveness. When you find your seat in class, you can be a ray of sunshine in that room or a dark cloud of anger. At practice, you can light up that space with joy or fill it with a bad mood. You get to choose.

Even on the days when you want to stay in bed with the covers over your head, you can ask God for the strength to put on Jesus. With Him, you can love your family, friends, classmates, teammates, and everyone you connect with.

God, help me wear Jesus every day!

THE BOOK OF ANSWERS

Your Word is a lamp to my feet and a light to my path.
PSALM 119:105

Sometimes we just need someone to explain things to us, or we need to find a book that gives us all of life's answers. The world is confusing, and people are even more confusing.

Maybe you struggle to understand your siblings or parents. Maybe boys puzzle you because you can't make sense of the things they do. Maybe you don't always get why your friends are fine one minute and then super moody the next. And maybe there are times you can't figure out why you act the way you do or say the things you say.

Wouldn't it be nice to have a handbook that explains it all?

Every time you pick up the Bible, that's exactly what you have. It's your Holy Handbook, and God has addressed every issue inside it. But to access its wisdom, you'll have to spend time reading it. You'll have to choose to open the Bible every day—and stick with it!

God, give me the strength and discipline to dig into Your Word every day so I can live wisely!

Believing without Seeing

You have never seen Him but you love Him. You cannot see Him now but you are putting your trust in Him. And you have joy so great that words cannot tell about it. You will get what your faith is looking for, which is to be saved from the punishment of sin.

1 PETER 1:8–9

Faith is believing in what you can't see, but it's hard to believe in someone you can't hang out with. It's hard building trust in someone whose face you don't get to see. And you may struggle to have confidence in someone you can't hug or high-five.

But Peter gives an exciting reason to have faith in God, even though you won't get to see Him with your eyes before you're in heaven. He says that if you have the courage to believe in Him, you'll have crazy amounts of joy on earth and get to live with God forever and ever in heaven. All of that for having the strength to believe without seeing.

God, help me have faith to trust You always! And thank You for inviting me to live with You forever in heaven!

courageous love pays off

*Live and work without pride. Be gentle and kind. Do not be
hard on others. Let love keep you from doing that. Work hard
to live together as one by the help of the Holy
Spirit. Then there will be peace.*
EPHESIANS 4:2–3

Loving others takes courage because it's so hard to do all
the time. When people are nice to us, loving them is easy. It
doesn't take much work to care for those who save us seats at
lunch, invite us to parties, or treat us kindly. But choosing to
love people who are mean or rude is another story.

God wants you to be gentle and kind, giving others grace
when they don't deserve it. He is asking you to put on your
big-girl pants and do everything you can to get along with
others. He wants you to be selfless and own your mistakes
rather than blame someone else. And you'll be able to live this
way by choosing to love those who are easy to love. . .and also
choosing to love those people who can be difficult.

God, help me have courageous love for everyone around me!

whose voice do you listen to?

"When the shepherd walks ahead of them,
they follow him because they know his voice."
JOHN 10:4

There are a lot of voices in the world today. And sometimes it gets confusing to know the right one to listen to because the messages are conflicting—they say different things.

There are the good ones that encourage you to be yourself and to be confident in who you are. They remind you that you're beautiful no matter what and that there's a powerful God who loves you. But there are also voices that say you must look a certain way, be in the right group at school, live in a certain neighborhood, or do things you know are wrong to be loved and accepted. The problem is that so often the loudest voices are the negatives ones.

Whose voices are you listening to these days? What keeps you from only listening to God's? How can you make sure you know the difference between His voice and the negative ones?

God, will You give me the strength to choose Your voice over
everyone else's? I only want to listen to You because
You always have my back.

why worry when you can pray?

"Which of you can make yourself a little taller by worrying?
If you cannot do that which is so little, why do you
worry about other things?"
LUKE 12:25–26

Worry does nothing to help you. Not one thing. Worrying about a test doesn't make you do better. Instead, it usually makes your brain stop working. Stressing out about a hard conversation doesn't do anything but make you sick to your stomach. Having anxiety about the report you have to give in front of the class does nothing but make you feel insecure. Worry is not your friend.

Rather than lose sleep over the hard things in your day, what if you prayed? While you're brushing your teeth, putting on shoes, or walking into school, why not tell God what has your stomach in knots? Ask Him to give you confidence and courage, strength and determination, and peace and comfort. Since we have prayer, we don't have to give in to worry.

What are you worried about right now? Take a minute and talk to God about it.

God, there are so many reasons I get worried.
Help me ditch the worry and trust You instead.

Jesus Has Your Back

*And so Jesus is able, now and forever, to save from the
punishment of sin all who come to God through Him
because He lives forever to pray for them.*
HEBREWS 7:25

Jesus always speaks up to God for you. Because you delight
Him so much, He chose to step out of heaven and down to
earth so He could die on the cross to save you from your sins.
This verse says that Jesus lives and acts as a mediator on your
behalf, and He prays for you continually. He is for you, He
loves you, and He cheers you on!

When you ask, Jesus gives you strength. He gives you
courage. He fills you with peace and joy. Jesus will heal you,
restore you, untangle you, direct you, and bring peace when
you're afraid. You may have lots of people on earth who love
you, but no one can love you the way Jesus can.

Whenever you feel lonely or unloved, think back on all
the ways Jesus proves your worth. Remember all the ways He
acts on your behalf. You are precious to Him!

God, thank You for Jesus!

look to god instead

*"Look to the Lord and ask for His strength.
Look to Him all the time."*
1 CHRONICLES 16:11

When you're in a hard situation, do you crumble and cry. . .or do you start to pray? When you fail at something, do you get angry and agitated. . .or do you talk to God? When it feels like the world is against you, do you scream and sob. . .or do you drop to your knees and give it to the Lord?

So often, our normal response is to freak out. We run to our besties or our parents, hoping they will fix things for us. Or we hide under the covers with a big bowl of ice cream, trying to fill our belly and wishing it would fill our heart too. We look for anything on earth that will make us feel better. But why don't we find the grit to look to God instead?

Courageous girl, God is for you! Bravely let Him know what you need, because He promises to help.

*God, You are so awesome. I want to look to
You for anything and everything.*

The Most Epic Fruit Salad Ever

*But the fruit that comes from having the Holy Spirit in our lives
is: love, joy, peace, not giving up, being kind, being good,
having faith, being gentle, and being the boss over our
own desires. The Law is not against these things.*
GALATIANS 5:22–23

What are your favorite fruits? Apples? Grapes? Bananas?
Strawberries? You'd probably have a hard time picking just
one because they're all yummy! Each has a unique flavor, and
when mixed together, they create one awesome fruit salad.

Because you're a Jesus girl, do you realize you have access
to a different kind of fruit? Galatians tells you what "fruits"—
godly characteristics—the Holy Spirit (God's Spirit) gives
you. When you say yes to Jesus, these fruits begin to grow in
you, and you can access them when you need them. Mixed
together, they make you a mature Christian who lives and
loves well.

What fruit do you need the most? What fruit of the
Spirit is the easiest for you? Remember that you can confidently ask God for help plucking these fruits whenever and
wherever.

God, thank You for creating in me the most epic fruit salad ever!

Follow His Steps

*The steps of a good man are led by the Lord. And He is happy
in his way. When he falls, he will not be thrown
down, because the Lord holds his hand.*

PSALM 37:23–24

Have you ever fallen down in front of a lot of people? Maybe
you tripped on the soccer field, or fell down the stairs at
school, or bumped into someone in the halls and fell flat on
your backside. It's so embarrassing when things like that happen and even harder to live through the giggles and com-
ments from those who saw it happen.

God knows we're human, and that means we will fall
down in other ways too. He knows we'll make bad choices
and do things we know are wrong. He knows we will make
sketchy decisions that will get us into trouble. But rather than
laugh or shame us, God is there to pick us up and set us on
the right path.

Courageously ask God to go before you so you can follow His steps. He will never lead you the wrong way.

God, I want to follow You all the days of my life.

The Only Perfect Thing

As for God, His way is perfect. The Word of the Lord has stood the test. He is a covering for all who go to Him for a safe place.
PSALM 18:30

◄◄❧

Nothing in this world is perfect: No parent (nope, not even your mom). No friend, classmate, or teammate. No teacher or youth leader. Nothing built or created. No plans or ideas. So, if you are looking for perfection from one of these, you're going to end up disappointed.

But there is a place you can find perfection.

Scripture tells us God's will and ways are perfect. It says His Word—the Bible—is perfect. And it teaches that His ability to care for us is perfect. But it takes courage to believe, especially because we are surrounded by people and things that let us down every day.

Do you struggle to trust God? Are you afraid He will let you down or not show up at all? Ask God to give you the faith to know He is always faithful and trustworthy.

*God, I know You're the only perfect One anywhere.
Give me the courage to trust You!*

Brave Enough to Believe

"Do not let your heart be troubled. You have put your trust in God, put your trust in Me also."

JOHN 14:1

In this passage of scripture, Jesus is comforting His followers. He's reminding them that He has their back so they can relax. And even though this reminder is from a long, long time ago, we can also be encouraged by His words today.

It's like Jesus is refocusing you. He is snapping His fingers in front of your sweet face to get your attention. He is reminding you that He knows your worries and is trustworthy to fix them.

Can you remember a time when you prayed about something, felt comforted and encouraged that you'd get through it, and then found yourself freaking out about it again? Rather than trusting God to mend your friendship or fix the situation at home, you started to worry again. You got scared.

Jesus is asking you to put your trust in Him and keep it there.

God, I'm sorry that I stopped trusting You. Please make me brave enough to believe in Your ability to fix the things that worry me.

STICKY JOY

"You are sad now. I will see you again and then your hearts
will be full of joy. No one can take your joy from you."
JOHN 16:22

You are the boss of you. And when it comes to certain things, you're the one who gets to make choices for yourself. You choose whether you get mad or offended when someone says rude things. You get to choose if you are friendly and kind or not. You are the one who decides what your attitude will be for today. And it's you who chooses if joy sticks to you or not.

But let's be honest. Sometimes, joy is hard to hold on to. It can start sliding away when you hear a mean rumor about yourself or when you do something embarrassing in front of a crowd. It can unstick when your parents ground you or you forgot the test was today. But sweet one, even with all of these joy killers, you can be brave and choose to let it stick to you instead.

Regardless of your situation, ask God for the courage to make joy stick.

God, help me have sticky joy no matter what!

prayer expectations

"Ask, and what you are asking for will be given to you.
Look, and what you are looking for you will find. Knock,
and the door you are knocking on will be opened to you."
MATTHEW 7:7

In this verse, Jesus is teaching us how to pray. He is making sure we understand that prayer isn't empty. Sometimes it can seem like our prayers hit the ceiling and bounce back down. We get frustrated because it feels like God isn't answering us quickly enough or isn't responding with what we desperately want. And there are times it makes us want to give up praying altogether because it just doesn't seem to be working.

But Jesus wants you to know that if you have the courage to really seek God, you'll find Him. If you boldly ask for things that don't go against His will for you, He'll give them. And if He says no to any of them, it's only because there's a better yes down the road.

God hears every prayer you pray, so don't give up until He answers.

God, give me strength to seek Your help even
when the answer doesn't come right away.

Attitude Is Everything

A glad heart is good medicine,
but a broken spirit dries up the bones.
PROVERBS 17:22

From the day you were born to the day you see Jesus face-to-face, you're going to face some hard times, mean people, and frustrating moments. It's just part of life, and no one gets through life without feeling broken at times. That's normal. It's to be expected. But you don't have to let yucky things ruin this glorious life!

No matter what life throws your way, you can stand up to it and be okay. You are brave, sweet girl! And attitude is everything.

The happiest people are the ones who look for the silver lining—the good things—when their situation looks ugly. It doesn't mean they don't hurt. They may be afraid. Chances are they'd rather hide under their blankets until things get easier. But rather than live broken, they choose to have a glad heart.

You're not a victim. Courageous girl, you are a victor!

God, I want to see the silver lining in everything.
Help me have the right attitude no matter what!

what Label Do You wear?

God is the One Who makes our faith and your faith strong in Christ.
He has set us apart for Himself. He has put His mark on us to show
we belong to Him. His Spirit is in our hearts to prove this.
2 CORINTHIANS 1:21–22

Do you ever feel like you're wearing an unflattering label, one that says ugly, stupid, or unlovable? And because you're sure everyone can see that invisible label stuck right to your forehead, it makes you feel insecure. You find yourself nervous that someone might notice the label and make fun of you. You're worried about being rejected and disliked. And rather than enjoy your time at school or with friends, you want to hide instead.

Well, the truth is that you do wear a label—a mark that God has placed on you to show you belong to Him. It's a label that tells how much you are loved, how treasured you are, and how much God delights in who you are! So be confident, because you wear it well.

God, remind me that I'm marked by You and that I'm
deeply loved regardless of what others think.

never alone

"No man will be able to stand against you all the days of your life.
I will be with you just as I have been with Moses. I will
be faithful to you and will not leave you alone."

JOSHUA 1:5

There's a big difference between being alone and being lonely. When you're alone, you still feel loved and valued. Maybe you need that alone time because it's how you recharge after being with friends all day. Maybe it's when you get your homework or chores done. But lonely is different.

You feel lonely when you believe lies that say you're not lovable. It's when you think no one wants to hang out with you because you're not good enough. It's when you feel left out by your friends, and it makes you question your awesomeness. Those lies of loneliness have the power to knock your self-confidence.

But you can have confidence in this truth: God will never, ever leave you. Even if all your friends ditch you, God never will. There will always be someone with you.

God, I need courage to keep my chin up when I feel alone
and to remember You're always with me!

Look at the God Things

Be full of joy always because you belong to the Lord.
Again I say, be full of joy!
PHILIPPIANS 4:4

There are plenty of reasons to not be joyful these days. Fights with friends, frustrations with parents, and fears about your grades. There are stresses with schedules, anger at coaches, and annoyances with your siblings. You may worry about a family problem or a disease someone is battling. There's anxiety about fitting in, standing out, and finding the right friends. You may be nervous about making the wrong decisions or not being strong enough to choose the right ones. Unfortunately, there are lots of ways sadness can creep into your heart.

Paul writes in Philippians that your ability to have joy requires one thing, and it's to know you belong to God. That alone should make joy explode in your heart! Because when you focus your attention on the hard things, you can't see the God things. But when you instead look at all the good things about God and how much He loves you, you can find the courage to look away from the things that steal your joy.

God, help me focus on the You things!

New Things

"See, I will do a new thing. It will begin happening now.
Will you not know about it? I will even make a road
in the wilderness, and rivers in the desert."
ISAIAH 43:19

This truth should encourage you! Sometimes we are desperate for God to do a new thing in our life because the situation we're currently in is so hard. We want a fresh start so we can put bad choices behind us and move on. We're ready to walk a new path with new friends or a new attitude. There are times we crave something new!

What do you need God to make fresh in your life? Do you need different friendships or a new semester to start? Do you need a new relationship with your parents or a better way to handle conflict? God is a God of new things, and you can boldly ask for His help whenever you need it.

God, I need help to see the new roads and rivers You're creating
for me. Just like You did for Isaiah, I am asking
You to do a new thing in my life today.

The Sound of Joy

How happy are the people who know the sound of joy!
They walk in the light of Your face, O Lord.
PSALM 89:15

Are you a complainer? If asked, would your family and friends say you're critical of others? Would they say you nitpick, finding the negatives in situations? Do you whine when you don't get your way or protest when Mom asks you to do chores? Is it easy for you to find fault in the ways others do things? Do you nag your friends or siblings? These are hard questions to face because sometimes we don't even know we're being that way.

But if you want to be happy and enjoy all that life has to offer, then learn to hear the sound of joy. Just what is that? It's the opposite of complaining.

Have the courage to look past the negatives and find the good things instead. With your relationships, your schoolwork, and your extracurricular activities. . .choose to focus on the positives so you can be joyful. And you'll be more fun to be around too!

God, I want to be a positive person and
spread joy to those around me!

Always the Same

Jesus Christ is the same yesterday and today and forever.
HEBREWS 13:8

One of the things we can be certain of is that change will happen. Everything in life changes. Think about it. Next year you'll be in a different grade or maybe a different school altogether. You may be taller and have longer hair, and you'll probably have to buy the next size up in clothes and shoes. Your group of friends may have some new members, and your team will look different too. Change happens.

But God never changes. He is always faithful, always trustworthy, always listening, always forgiving, and His love for you never changes. God is the One you can cling to when change gets scary, because you know He will keep you steady. He will always be 100 percent devoted to you, ready to help when you ask.

The Lord will always be there to help you walk through the changes you'll face in life. Ask, and He will give you the strength to do it well.

God, change is hard for me because it's scary.
Would You make me brave and help me accept new things?

The Waiting Game

"The Lord is my share," says my soul, "so I have hope in Him."
The Lord is good to those who wait for Him, to the one who
looks for Him. It is good that one should be quiet and
wait for the saving power of the Lord.
LAMENTATIONS 3:24–26

No one likes to wait. We want what we want right now, don't we? We want the fight to be over without talking it through. We want grades to change now without having to study more. We're impatient that summer break is months away and cranky that we're grounded for another week. We pray, asking God to fix the situation or heal our broken heart. And so often, the answers come slow, and we think we'll burst because being patient is excruciating.

But this passage of scripture says God is good to those who wait for Him. He loves it when we trust, giving Him space to work things out for us. And God will reward us for waiting on Him.

God, I need strength to overcome my impatience.
Help me trust that You hear me and are working on it.

The Payoff for Patience

But they who wait upon the Lord will get new strength. They will rise up with wings like eagles. They will run and not get tired. They will walk and not become weak.

ISAIAH 40:31

In this verse, God is making a very powerful promise. He is telling you the payoff for being patient and choosing to trust that He is making a way for you. God is giving you His word that your patience will bring an awesome benefit: endurance.

What are some of the ways impatience gets the best of you? Do you throw a temper tantrum? Have a pity party? Do you become cranky, making sure everyone pays for your frustration?

How would things be different if you instead decided to bravely wait for God to do what only God can do? And if that big dose of strength you needed to deal with a tough situation was the payoff for choosing to trust God, would you?

God's got this. Your job is to trust Him as you wait.

God, help me remember how faithful You are.
Give me patience as I wait on You.

A Life Full of Seasons

*There is a special time for everything. There is a time
for everything that happens under heaven.*

ECCLESIASTES 3:1

Life flows in seasons. There are times when it seems everything is clicking, and things feel exciting and easy. Friendships are strong, your family is connecting, and you're content. There isn't much drama or sadness, just happy moments that make your heart feel full. But there are also times when you're overwhelmed by life. Situations are hard and relationships are frustrating, and you just want to curl up in your favorite blanket and cry.

Be ready, courageous girl. Be brave. Because life will often be a roller-coaster ride full of ups and downs. It will be full of good and bad, beautiful and painful. But the one constant will be God. He will be with you through it all. He will cheer you on and wipe away every tear you cry because God is for you and always with you.

It will take courage, but the Lord will give it to you when you need it.

God, help me lean on You in all the seasons I'll walk through.

Better Than Anything Else

O taste and see that the Lord is good.
How happy is the man who trusts in Him!
PSALM 34:8

What are your favorite foods? Ice cream or pizza? Steak or chicken alfredo? Banana bread or Caesar salad? Sushi or chili? Think about how much you look forward to eating those foods and how they put a huge smile on your face. Now, remember what it tastes like when you take that first bite. You probably close your eyes and breathe out with pleasure, maybe even sighing loud enough so those around can hear. And remember how happy you are once you're full.

That's the kind of reaction we should have about God. We should crave time with Him and think about our heavenly Father with excitement. We should look forward to connecting and feel happy when we do. Because He is so good—better than anything the world can offer—our heart should be full when we spend time with Him.

Put God at the top of your menu every day. He is better than anything else!

God, I'm determined to crave a relationship
with You above all other things.

YOU ARE SEEN

God sees you. He sees every tear you cry, and He knows all the ways your sweet heart gets broken. God sees those things that bring you joy. He is cheering you on as you take courageous steps forward into tough situations. He knows what scares you. He sees those circumstances that make you feel small. God is fully aware of the people who encourage you and the ones who hurt your feelings. He knows what you need even before you do and has already determined a way to help.

Sometimes we feel unseen even by our closest friends and family. We feel like no one really knows how we're feeling or what we're thinking. We decide we're all alone. But that's not true, and we can ask God for the confidence to believe that He sees inside our heart and knows everything that's going on.

*God, thank You for knowing me like You do.
Remind me I'm not alone and that You always see me.*

COURAGEOUS ASKS

God is able to do much more than we ask or think through His power working in us.
EPHESIANS 3:20

God's power and ability are endless. Think about it. He can do anything He wants. God can make anything happen at any time. And He can dream bigger than we can ever imagine. We may ask for the cupcake, but He can give us the entire bakery!

What do you need God to do? Where do you need Him to show up in your life? What are you asking Him for? This is your challenge, to ask for more. Ask bigger. Ask for things only God can make happen. Be courageous in your prayers, and boldly ask Him for your heart's desire.

At the same time, be brave enough to accept God's answer. Sometimes He answers over and above what we asked, and other times He requires us to wait as He lines things up. And there are also times His answer is no because there is something better right around the corner. Regardless, be fearless in your asks.

God, help me be fearless and bold in the prayers I pray to You!

what are you focusing on?

We do not look at the things that can be seen. We look at the things that cannot be seen. The things that can be seen will come to an end. But the things that cannot be seen will last forever.

2 CORINTHIANS 4:18

This verse offers a powerful tip. It's saying a key to living a happy life is to not focus on the problems we face. Rather than freak out that our family is in crisis or that we're moving across the country, we instead focus on God. We say, "This is scary, but I trust that whatever You're doing is for the best!"

Refocusing isn't easy, especially when everything seems to be going wrong. It's hard to trust when your grades are failing, your friendships are frustrating, and your motivation is falling apart. It's hard to stay out of the drama! But if you can find the courage to step back, take a deep breath, and talk to God about it, you'll be able to focus on the right things.

God, help me keep my eyes on You when life gets hard.
And help me trust that You have everything under control!

when are you quiet?

*"All of you be quiet before the Lord.
For He is coming from His holy place."*
ZECHARIAH 2:13

The world is loud, and many of us like it that way. We love our music and the laughter from our friends. We love to watch our favorite shows and sit around the dinner table talking with our family. Youth group and team sports are times when we interact with others, and before we go to sleep, we're on our phones squeezing out every last bit of conversation.

But do you ever make time to sit quietly with God? Without music or conversation, do you find moments when it's just you and God? He has so much to say to you, but it requires you to listen for His voice. If your attention is always somewhere else, how will you hear Him?

Starting today, why not schedule time to sit in silence with God and listen for His voice? He has things to say. Will you listen?

God, help me be firm in my commitment to spend time with You quietly. Please meet me there and speak to my heart.

The Power to Meet Needs

He lets me rest in fields of green grass. He leads me beside the quiet waters. He makes me strong again. He leads me in the way of living right with Himself which brings honor to His name.
PSALM 23:2–3

The Twenty-Third Psalm is one of the most popular passages of scripture in the Bible because it shows us God's power to meet our needs. Every one of us has moments when we desperately need what these verses offer. Reread the verses out loud. Which parts speak to you the most? Why?

It's important to remember that no matter your age, race, location, or anything else, God is always available. He doesn't listen to one person before another person because He doesn't have to. When you cry out to Him, you have 100 percent of His attention. And somehow at the very same time, anyone who prays to God also has His full attention.

That means when you need rest, direction, courage, or strength, God hears you the moment you ask Him for it.

*God, thank You for always being there
to meet every one of my needs.*

created and molded

*But now, O Lord, You are our Father. We are the clay,
and You are our pot maker. All of us are the work of Your hand.*
ISAIAH 64:8

God created you. Period. If you believe the Bible to be completely true, then settle this fact in your mind today. God is the One who thought you up. He decided what you would look like, when and where you'd be born, what family you would grow up in, and all the talents He'd give to you. God took His time to form you just right.

Even now, God continues to mold you into the person He has planned for all along. Every hard thing you face, God uses for your benefit. And even the joy-filled times are used to develop you too. From friend drama to being cast as the lead in the school play, God is directly involved in your life. And now that you understand He has His fingers in every part of your life, you can confidently choose to trust Him no matter what.

Heavenly Father, thank You for making me. . .me!

wherever you go

*"See, I am with you. I will care for you everywhere you go.
And I will bring you again to this land. For I will not leave
you until I have done all the things I promised you."*
GENESIS 28:15

There are few people who promise to be with you through thick and thin. Most parents would make that kind of pledge. So would your bestie. There might also be a mentor or two or a small-group leader. But no one can totally make that promise because life is so unpredictable.

That's why God's promise to be with you everywhere you go is so awesome! Without fail, you can always count on God to be available when you need Him. He will always care for you and give you the things you need to get through your day. And there is nothing you can do to make Him mad enough to leave you. God is incapable of abandoning you.

Find time today to tell God what this promise means to you.

*God, what would I do without You?
I'm so glad You will never leave me.*

who do you trust more?

"Good will come to the man who trusts in the Lord, and whose hope is in the Lord. He will be like a tree planted by the water, that sends out its roots by the river. It will not be afraid when the heat comes but its leaves will be green. It will not be troubled in a dry year, or stop giving fruit."
JEREMIAH 17:7–8

Every day, you have a choice to make. You can put your trust in people, or you can instead decide to trust God. And honestly, it's a hard choice to make. But when you put your faith in God, not only will you grow, but you'll have the strength and courage necessary to take the next right step.

This passage in Jeremiah gives the perfect example of what trusting God looks like and how having faith saves you. Just like the tree planted by the water, you will have access to resources to help you get through the dramatic moments of life. And that's something only God can give you.

God, give me the boldness I need to trust You over anyone else. You are faithful!

Blessing from waiting

I did not give up waiting for the Lord. And He turned to me and heard my cry. He brought me up out of the hole of danger, out of the mud and clay. He set my feet on a rock, making my feet sure.
PSALM 40:1–2

What kind of trials and hard times have you faced? We've all had something. Maybe it was the loss of a family member or friend, fear that you might be sick, rejection from someone you love, or horrible consequences from a bad choice. Everyone has been in the pit before, just waiting and hoping to be rescued. And chances are those pits have taught you some good things.

It's the time we spend waiting in those hard places that brings about blessings. We become stronger or smarter. We learn to be more compassionate and loving. We find a deeper faith in God. Or we realize we're braver than we thought. Sometimes God allows the pit to be a classroom only because He will use it to help us grow. And when the timing is perfect, He pulls us from it.

God, help me see the blessings that come from waiting.

You're Kind of a Big Deal

*But you are a chosen group of people. You are the King's religious
leaders. You are a holy nation. You belong to God. He has done
this for you so you can tell others how God has called
you out of darkness into His great light.*

1 PETER 2:9

Courageous girl, you are kind of a big deal. Think about it:
Your Father is the Creator of the heavens and earth. He is
the King of kings and the Lord of lords. He is and always
has been. And there is none greater than God. And that
makes you royalty.

According to Peter, you are chosen. That means handpicked. You are holy because you belong to God and He is
holy. And He has given you a voice to tell others about what
He has done in your life. You're His spokesperson.

Be brave enough to walk in the truth. Others might try
to cut you down and make you feel worthless, but remember
who you are. Because of God, you are kind of a big deal.

*God, thank You for being such an amazing
heavenly Father! I love You so much.*

Time to Move On

*No, Christian brothers, I do not have that life yet. But I do one
thing. I forget everything that is behind me and look forward
to that which is ahead of me. My eyes are on the crown.
I want to win the race and get the crown of God's
call from heaven through Christ Jesus.*

PHILIPPIANS 3:13-14

It's time to let go of what you have done and instead grab
on to what God is doing in your life moving forward.
We've all done shameful things and have made wrong
choices. We've all been mean to friends and rude to family
members. We may have cheated on a test or stolen something from a store without getting caught. But having faith
and trusting in God gives us the ability to leave those in
the past and focus on our relationship with Jesus.

Ask God for the courage to not dwell on the ways you've
failed. Because of Jesus' death on the cross, you've been forgiven for every bad choice. Now it's time to move forward
and concentrate on building a strong relationship with Jesus.

God, thank You for fresh beginnings!

Take pride in your work

Whatever work you do, do it with all your heart.
Do it for the Lord and not for men.
COLOSSIANS 3:23

You were created to work—we all were. When God thought you up, He decided what gifts and talents you would get and how they would benefit those around you. It's easy to grumble about work, whether it's schoolwork or a job you're paid to do. Sometimes we'd rather be doing anything but the work right in front of us. But if you look at work as an act of worship instead, it could change your attitude.

Ask God to help you value working. Take pride in making good grades, and care about the papers you have to write. Put all your effort into the class presentation, and be prepared for the game. Memorize your part in the play, and perfect your choir or band solo. Do these things to make God proud and to show Him you are thankful for the skills He has trusted you with.

God, I want to honor You in my work.
Thanks for blessing me with the ability to do things well.

The Focus of Life

"I am the Vine and you are the branches. Get your life from Me. Then I will live in you and you will give much fruit. You can do nothing without Me."

JOHN 15:5

There are lots of people who think being good is the goal of life. In their own strength, they work hard to treat people kindly, save seats for friends at lunch, volunteer at vacation Bible school, and offer to be the teacher's helper in class. While those things are worthwhile, alone they won't make your life perfect. Even more, your strength will eventually run out, and you'll become bitter that you're having to work so hard.

But Jesus says the focus of your life should be having a relationship with Him. It's from that connection that we can bless and serve others. We will be able to access His strength and grace to be kind to those around us. We can access His courage to love those who are hard to love and forgive those who are hard to forgive. Staying close to Jesus is how we live a beautiful and fulfilling life.

God, I'm choosing to stick with You!

what anchors you?

This hope is a safe anchor for our souls. It will never move. This hope goes into the Holiest Place of All behind the curtain of heaven.
HEBREWS 6:19

Who are the anchors in your life? You know, the people who hold you steady. Is it your friends? Your parents? Maybe an older sibling or a small-group leader. Maybe an aunt or uncle. Or maybe you anchor yourself to the idea of being perfect or being an overachiever. We all rely on different anchors to help us make sense of this crazy world.

But God is the only safe anchor because we can confidently place our hope in Him. We can trust that He will always keep us close and safe. He will be there whenever we need help or wisdom, courage or strength, peace or comfort. While we may be loved by some pretty awesome people here on earth, it's God's love that's able to move mountains on our behalf. And when we make the bold decision to tie our life to Him, He will protect us.

God, my hope is anchored in You.
Help me stay connected to You above anyone else.

Desperate Prayers

I call to You from the end of the earth when my heart is weak.
Lead me to the rock that is higher than I. For You have been
a safe place for me, a tower of strength where I am safe from
those who fight against me. Let me live in Your tent forever.
Let me be safe under the covering of Your wings.
Psalm 61:2–4

Can you hear the writer's desperation in this verse? It's obvious he's in a pretty rough spot and in need of God's help. Can you relate?

Think back to a time when you were at the end of your rope. Maybe you were in an epic fight with your parents and felt unheard. Maybe there was a rumor at school that wouldn't die down and you were embarrassed. Maybe your best efforts in class weren't paying off and your grade suffered. Maybe you're in a desperate place right now.

If there's anything to learn from the psalmist, it's that God is willing and able to help when you need it, but you have to be courageous enough to reach out.

God, hear my desperate prayers and help me. I need You.

It's a Sure Thing

"Do not fear, for I am with you. Do not be afraid, for I am your God. I will give you strength, and for sure I will help you. Yes, I will hold you up with My right hand that is right and good."
ISAIAH 41:10

God promises to step in when we ask. Where do you need His help today? Are you struggling and scared? Are your feelings hurt? Do you need courage or wisdom to do the next right thing? Are you feeling weak? Unlovable or unlikable? Unworthy? Overwhelmed? Stressed-out? Sometimes this life just beats us up. But sweet one, never forget that God sees you right where you are.

Did you notice in today's verse where He says He will "for sure" help when we need it? That means He will without a doubt be there for you. It means nothing will stop God from getting involved. He is ready and willing to act on your behalf. Your challenge is to be fearless in asking for His help.

God, I know You're there for me, but sometimes I struggle to ask for help. Please give me the courage to reach out.

you can go to god for anything

*Let us go with complete trust to the throne of God.
We will receive His loving-kindness and have His
loving-favor to help us whenever we need it.*
HEBREWS 4:16

You can go to God for anything, at any time, no matter what. Even more, you can pray to Him with complete trust, knowing that He will hear you and respond. Your friends and family may have the same good intentions because they love you so much, but only God can meet your needs 100 percent of the time. Only God is available right when you need Him. And He is the One who holds every answer and solution in His hands.

So, what do you need from God today? More patience with your siblings? Compassion for that annoying classmate who won't give you space? Wisdom to know how to talk to your mom about something that's bothering you? Confidence for the big game? Courage to stand up for yourself? Ask God. He's waiting to hear from you.

God, I need Your help today. Thank You that I can talk to You about anything and that You already have the answers I need.

what to do when others are mean

My times are in Your hands. Free me from the hands of those who hate me, and from those who try to hurt me. Make Your face shine upon Your servant. Save me in Your loving-kindness.
PSALM 31:15–16

Life can be hard, and people can be so mean, leaving you feeling hopeless, like things will never be okay. It's difficult to understand how people can be so hurtful, especially when it's on purpose. And it leaves us feeling unloved and scared.

One of the best things to do when you're overwhelmed by the meanness of others is pray. God is able to change the situation as well as the hearts of people trying to hurt you. He can make it stop. And because God sees everything, there is nothing happening to you that He's missed. He knows exactly what's going on, and God is waiting for you to ask for His help. Be bold and tell God what you're feeling and what you need. He's listening.

God, I am struggling. I'm sad about how others are treating me. I need Your help right now.

prayer: a weapon against lies

*Let the lying lips be quiet. For they speak with
pride and hate those who do right and good.*

PSALM 31:18

Few things hurt more than having lies spread about you.
Whether it's a friend betraying you or someone you barely
know starting the rumor, lies cut deep. And they usually
spread like a wildfire, circulating from one person to the next
at record speeds. Even more, it's so hurtful that people who
know you would choose to believe whatever they're told. But
the hardest part may be finding the courage to walk the halls
when you know others are gossiping about you.

People usually talk bad about one another because
doing so makes them feel better about themselves. They
fuel mean-spirited rumors because they're jealous or angry.
And unfortunately, at some point in your life—if you haven't
already—you will be the victim of a liar.

But there's hope. Prayer is a weapon you can use anytime,
and sometimes it takes everything you've got to step out of
the hurt to pray to the Healer. But when you do, God will
help.

God, I'm hurting. Please give me peace and strength.

who's the boss?

If your sinful old self is the boss over your mind, it leads
to death. But if the Holy Spirit is the boss over
your mind, it leads to life and peace.
ROMANS 8:6

Keeping your thoughts in check is a full-time job. It's easy
to focus on bad things happening rather than what's going
right. The frustrating moments can easily overshadow the
good ones. Think about it. If five friends compliment you on
your outfit and just one person says it's ugly, which one do
you remember?

God wants to be the boss of your mind. He wants you
to listen to His voice above all else. Instead of letting your
mind focus on all the negatives in the situations you're facing,
choose to look for where God is moving. Be courageous and
stand up to those bad thoughts. Tell them to pack their bags
and leave. Don't let them be the boss of your mind, because
they will ruin your day.

What bad thoughts do you need to kick to the curb?

God, please be the boss of my thoughts and
show me the ones I need to let go of right now.

Did You Check With God?

There are many plans in a man's heart,
but it is the Lord's plan that will stand.
PROVERBS 19:21

This verse isn't suggesting that you not make plans. Truth is, it's important to take steps forward and have hopes and dreams for the future.

There may be a certain college you want to go to or places you want to travel to when you get older. You may have a career in mind, like becoming a lawyer, nurse, singer, or dancer. God gave you a brilliant mind to think for yourself and make plans, and He also gave you a big dose of hope for things to come. Part of growing up is learning how to make wise choices.

But what this verse is suggesting is that you hold these plans loosely because God may have something else in mind. Something better. Something bigger. Something different. Your challenge is to be confident enough to make plans, faithful enough to ask God if He agrees, and courageous enough to set them aside if God shows you another path.

God, I am excited for my future!
And I want to make decisions about it with You!

It Doesn't Matter What They Think

The fear of man brings a trap,
but he who trusts in the Lord will be honored.

PROVERBS 29:25

It's easy to worry about what others think. We become people pleasers because we want to be liked. Our heart can ache for the seal of approval from certain people. We become overwhelmed by focusing our time and energy on making sure we're loved by everyone around us. It's exhausting. Even more, the writer of Proverbs 29:25 tells us that worrying too much about the opinions of others is a trap.

Based on your own life, can you see that? Can you recall times you cared more about what *they* thought rather than courageously following what God was asking of you? The writer goes on to say that if you will boldly trust God and follow His way instead, He will honor you. In other words, if you make the hard choice to care about God's will over the approval of anyone else, you'll be rewarded. It takes guts and grit, but you can do it.

God, give me courage to not care so
much about what others think.

God Protects His Girls

"The robber comes only to steal and to kill and to destroy. I came so they might have life, a great full life."
JOHN 10:10

There is an Enemy who hates you. *Hate* is a pretty strong word, but it's true. The devil has plans for your life, and they are to steal your happiness, kill your joy, and destroy your hope. Don't let that scare you, courageous girl. Remember, you're the daughter of the Most High King, who has amazing plans for your future! But you need knowledge so you understand what the devil wants for you.

When you say yes to becoming a Jesus girl, you're protected by Him. It doesn't mean life will be perfect and without yucky times and messy situations, but it does mean that when you courageously hold on to Jesus, you are a victor—not a victim. No matter what you face—mean girls, bad grades, divorced parents, or a scary sickness—with Jesus you win because He will make the bad things work in your favor.

God, help me be brave when I am overwhelmed by the devil's plans. I trust You!

scared of the Dark?

*This is what we heard Him tell us. We are passing it on
to you. God is light. There is no darkness in Him.*

1 John 1:5

Are you scared of the dark? Does it make you feel anxious or
all alone? When your parents say good night and turn off the
light as they leave your room at bedtime, does the darkness
feel overwhelming? It's okay if it does. The dark can cause
fear, worry, and anxiety.

You may be afraid of the literal dark, but you can also be
scared of those dark times in life when you're overwhelmed.
Fights, fears, and frustrations have a way of blocking the light
right out of life.

But God is light. He's the opposite of the dark. There's
not one bit of blackness in Him. Nothing negative, hurtful,
scary, or mean-spirited. So when you get scared, the best
thing you can do is pray because when you do, your prayers
are bringing light into those dark places. Ask Him to shine
His light into your heart and your situation.

*God, Your light makes me fearless.
Please help me look to You when I am scared.*

The old switcheroo

"You planned to do a bad thing to me. But God planned it for good, to make it happen that many people should be kept alive, as they are today."

GENESIS 50:20

This verse should make you smile ear to ear. It's the hope you can hold on to when bad things happen to you. When mean girls try to make your life miserable, when hurtful rumors are being spread about you, or when someone is picking on you, remember that their mean-spirited plans will fail in the end.

God promises to take all the cruel intentions of others and do a switcheroo. Sure, it might upset you right now, but good will eventually come from it. Maybe the mean girls will make you more confident, the rumors might help you become more courageous, and the one picking on you may become your best friend. Yes, God is capable of changing any situation to work in your favor. Your job is to trust Him to be faithful when you ask for His help.

God, when people do things to hurt me on purpose, remind me that You'll use it for good things.

God Comforts

*Yes, even if I walk through the valley of the shadow of death,
I will not be afraid of anything, because You are with me.
You have a walking stick with which to guide and
one with which to help. These comfort me.*

PSALM 23:4

Comfort is one of the sweetest gifts that God makes available to us, because let's be honest, life is hard. Sometimes it feels like we're constantly dealing with difficult or frustrating things, and that stirs up fear and anxiety.

We worry we'll never fit in at the new school, scared they won't like us. We're afraid to embarrass ourselves during the class presentation, terrified we'd never live it down. We fear rejection from our friends or betrayal from someone we love and trust, and our heart is stirred up and troubled.

God isn't okay with that, so He promises to bring comfort right when we need it the most. Courageous girl, ask for it. Whenever your heart feels anxious, no matter where you are, boldly ask God to comfort you. . .and He will.

*God, I'm going to stand up for myself
and ask for Your help when I need it.*

Give Yourself a Break

But as for me, I will watch for the Lord. I will wait for the God Who saves me. My God will hear me.
MICAH 7:7

Give yourself a break. You don't have to be perfect. Chances are the only one expecting perfection from you. . .is you. There's no reason to beat yourself up for being human. God made you, and He thinks you're pretty amazing even when you mess up.

Now, that's not an excuse for bad behavior. Instead, it's a reminder that you aren't expected to have it all together. There is grace for you! Ask God for the courage to accept that you're flawed and lovable at the same time.

Throughout your life, you're going to make countless mistakes. We all will. But God promises to be with you the whole time. Your Father in heaven won't leave you or forsake you because you do something wrong. And when you do mess up, ask God for help and forgiveness, and watch for Him to make things right.

God, thank You for letting me be imperfect.
Give me the confidence to accept it myself.

Hindsight Is Twenty-Twenty

*We want you to know, Christian brothers, of the trouble we had
in the countries of Asia. The load was so heavy we did not have the
strength to keep going. At times we did not think we could live.
We thought we would die. This happened so we would not put
our trust in ourselves, but in God Who raises the dead.*

2 CORINTHIANS 1:8–9

In today's verse, Paul is on the other side of his struggles in
Asia, which gave him the ability to look back and see the
bigger picture. Have you ever heard the phrase "Hindsight
is twenty-twenty"? Simply put, it means that when you look
back at a situation, you're able to understand it better now
than when you were right in the middle of it.

Can you think of a tough situation that made sense once
it was over? Something with a friend? A parent? A teacher?
Maybe God allowed that hard moment because He used it to
open your eyes or your heart to Him.

*God, give me the courage to learn from my
circumstances and see You in them.*

The safest place to be

So give yourselves to God. Stand against the devil and he will run away from you. Come close to God and He will come close to you. Wash your hands, you sinners. Clean up your hearts, you who want to follow the sinful ways of the world and God at the same time.

JAMES 4:7–8

The safest place for you to be is with God. You find that closeness when you pray to Him, read the Bible, listen to praise music, and spend quiet time listening for His voice. He is your safe place when things feel scary and overwhelming. And when it seems everything is falling apart, tucking away with God is the best place to ride out the storms.

He will give you courage so you don't give in to the devil's tricky plans. He will give you strength to face every challenge that comes your way. He will give you bravery to stand up for yourself. And God will give you determination to do the right things.

God, with Your help I can stand strong against the devil's plans. You're my safe place.

The weapons of strength and peace

The Lord will give strength to His people.
The Lord will give His people peace.
PSALM 29:11

God promises that He will give you strength and peace, two very powerful weapons to have in your arsenal. Strength is what gives you courage to do the next right thing, and it's peace that tells your heart that things will be okay. It whispers that God is with you.

Can you think of a situation you're in right now where you need both of these? Maybe it's frustration with a teammate or coach, or maybe a friendship feels unsteady. Maybe there's tension at home, and it has you worried and confused about what to do. Maybe you need to speak up for yourself but are scared it might backfire instead of help. Tell God how you're feeling, and ask Him to bring strength and peace.

You may really want to hide away and try to ignore the things that stress you out, but God wants you to grab hold of these weapons so you can thrive!

God, I'm so glad I can have strength and peace!
Would You give me the right dose of each at the right time?

You Are a Light

Jesus spoke to all the people, saying, "I am the Light of the world. Anyone who follows Me will not walk in darkness. He will have the Light of Life."

JOHN 8:12

You are a light. God has given you the ability to shine Him into the world. That means your words and your actions can be so amazing that those around you want to know your secret. They'll want to be your friend because you make them feel good. They'll be drawn to your kindness and courage, they'll see your wisdom and strength, and they'll want that for themselves.

Think of three people who need God in their life. Is it one of your friends who is struggling with self-worth? Is it a new kid desperate for someone to hang out with? Is it a sibling making bad choices or a parent trying to fix everything on their own? Ask God what you can do to shine Him into their life. Think of ways you can be a light for them.

God, give me the eyes to see people who need to know about You, and give me the courage to shine!

you're in good Hands

"I am the First and the Last. I am the beginning and the end."
REVELATION 22:13

Read today's verse out loud. What a powerful reminder that God always has been and will always be. He is at the start and the finish line and everything in between. There is no place He can't go or space He can't fill. He is fully present, fully available, fully involved. There is nothing and no one bigger or better than God.

So, what does this mean for you? It means you're in good hands. It means there is nothing you're dealing with that God cannot fix or help with. He has the unique ability to understand your struggle from every angle and has already made a way for you. It means you can take a deep breath knowing He has everything you need right in this moment. God has you, courageous girl.

How does this truth make you feel? How does it change how you see hard times? What does God want you to know?

_____

God, it makes me feel good to know You have everything under control. Give me courage to trust You when hard times hit.

DO YOU DOUBT GOD'S GREATNESS?

The Lord is great and our praise to Him should be great. He is too
great for anyone to understand. Families of this time will praise
Your works to the families-to-come. They will tell about Your
powerful acts. I will think about the shining-greatness of Your
power and about Your great works. Men will speak of Your
powerful acts that fill us with fear. And I will tell of Your greatness.
PSALM 145:3–6

Did you notice the word *great* is mentioned six times in today's verses? It's obvious the writer wants to make that truth clear—the truth that God is great. Why do you think he's so desperate for us to know it? Maybe it's because there are times when we doubt it.

It's hard to stay positive about God when life goes wrong. When everything seems to be falling apart, we often question God's goodness. We wonder why He doesn't save us from the mess or make relationships easier.

But we don't often get those answers. Instead, we need to find the courage to believe God is great no matter what.

God, I know You are great!

Hold Tight to the Truth

As you have put your trust in Christ Jesus the Lord to save you from the punishment of sin, now let Him lead you in every step. Have your roots planted deep in Christ. Grow in Him. Get your strength from Him. Let Him make you strong in the faith as you have been taught. Your life should be full of thanks to Him.
COLOSSIANS 2:6–7

God has plans for your life, ones He thought up before the creation of the world, and He will equip you to walk them out. That means God will give you everything you need to do what He's planned, and He's promised to be with you every step of the way. When He thought you up, God filled you with skills and talents that would grow and mature into awesomeness. There's no doubt you are a rock star!

Don't let anything take that from you. Remember, God created you to be unique on purpose, and the strength you need to thrive comes from God alone. Have the courage to hold that truth tightly.

God, help me grow in You. Help my faith be strong.
Help me trust You always.

Are You Angry at God?

"Agree with God, and be at peace with Him.
Then good will come to you."

JOB 22:21

When bad things happen, so often we get mad at God. We blame Him for all the things that have gone wrong. We decide He doesn't really love us or He doesn't see us, or we think He is a mean god. While those kinds of thoughts may be normal when our heart is breaking, they are not reality.

God can take your anger. If you're struggling with frustration toward Him right now, tell Him. He's big enough to handle it and willing to hear the things you're feeling. And once you get it all out, once you put it all on the table, God will be ready to put His peace in your heart.

Don't let another day go by without talking to Him. It may take every bit of courage in you, but you are free to confidently share your honest feelings because nothing you say will ever change how much He loves you.

God, I want to live at peace with You!
Would You help me work through my anger?

Be Bold in Your Faith

Then Nebuchadnezzar became very angry and called for Shadrach,
Meshach, and Abed-nego. And they were brought to the king.
Nebuchadnezzar said to them, "Is it true, Shadrach, Meshach and
Abed-nego, that you do not serve my gods or worship the object of
gold that I have set up? Now if you are ready to get down on your
knees and worship the object I have made when you hear the sound
of the horns and harps and all kinds of music, very well. But if
you will not worship, you will be thrown at once into the fire.
And what god is able to save you from my hands?"

DANIEL 3:13–15

It's hard to stand strong when others think your faith is silly.
We don't want to be made fun of, so we keep our belief in
God tucked away so no one can see it.

But God is calling you to be a modern-day Shadrach,
Meshach, and Abed-nego and to be bold about your relation-
ship with Him. It's never something to be ashamed about.
No. It's something to be confident and proud of.

God, I am not going to hide how much I love You anymore!

Faith under pressure

*"If we are thrown into the fire, our God Whom we serve is able
to save us from it. And He will save us from your hand, O king.
But even if He does not, we want you to know, O king,
that we will not serve your gods or worship the
object of gold that you have set up."*
DANIEL 3:17–18

Yesterday we read how the king threatened to throw Shadrach, Meshach, and Abed-nego in the fire for not worshipping him. We learned about the bold faith these three carried in their hearts. Today we watch them walk it out.

It's one thing to believe and another thing to believe under pressure. Just like these men did, we have to trust God's plan on such a deep level. They were going to love God whether He saved them from the fire or not. Their faith was solid.

What about you? Do you have a "no matter what" faith? It takes guts to trust God regardless of when or how He answers your prayers. Ask Him for faith under pressure so it can't be shaken.

God, I choose to trust You no matter what.

Faith in the Middle

Then they took him out of the city and threw stones at him.
The men who were throwing the stones laid their coats down in
front of a young man named Saul. While they threw stones at
Stephen, he prayed, "Lord Jesus, receive my spirit." After that he fell
on his knees and cried out with a loud voice, "Lord, do not hold
this sin against them." When he had said this, he died.
ACTS 7:58–60

Stephen was stoned to death for his faith. He had been encouraging others to follow the Lord, and it made some religious leaders angry, so they dragged him out of the city and threw rocks at him until he died.

You'll probably never see something so brutal happen just for believing, but you may be made fun of for being a Jesus girl. That's okay. People can be mean. But find the courage to be fearless when the mocking comes, having strong faith in the middle of the mean words. Don't allow anyone to make you turn your back on God, because He promises to never turn His back on you.

God, I am Your girl. I will be fearless in my faith!

worry is a waste of time

Jesus said to His followers, "Because of this, I say to you, do not worry about your life, what you are going to eat. Do not worry about your body, what you are going to wear. Life is worth more than food. The body is worth more than clothes."
LUKE 12:22–23

Do you worry? It's easy to get freaked out about little things and big things alike. We're worried because we're afraid something bad will happen. We imagine horrible outcomes and endings, and it keeps us awake at night. It makes it hard to focus at school. Worry can feel overwhelming.

But Jesus tells us worry doesn't belong in our life. He says it's a waste of our time because we end up focusing on the *what if* rather than the *what is*. If we truly trust God, we shouldn't worry. Instead, we must bravely choose to trust He'll work it all out—even the things that feel scary.

Where do you need to trust God today?

God, worry is a waste of time, and I need Your help to get rid of it. Help me trust You more!

Praise Is Powerful

*Go into His gates giving thanks and into His holy place
with praise. Give thanks to Him. Honor His name.*
PSALM 100:4

When you take time to thank God for the things He has done in your life, it's powerful. Being grateful for who He is makes a difference in your heart. It builds trust and courage for what's ahead. Praise is a game changer because it shifts your attitude and your focus.

Think about it. How can you feel hopeless about your family situation when you're busy thanking God for all He is preparing to do? If you're focused on God's promise to never leave you, how can you feel alone? And being grateful for His strength gives you the freedom to trust He is working things out.

Take time today to thank God for being, well, God. Thank Him for having a perfect track record in your life, and tell God you're trusting Him now. Remind yourself of all the ways He's shown up and helped you with your friendships, fears, and insecurities. It helps you, and it will delight God!

*God, You're pretty amazing,
and I am grateful You are in my life!*

Stepping In with Truth

So Manoah said to his wife, "We will die for sure. For we have seen God." But his wife said to him, "If the Lord had wanted to kill us, He would not have received a burnt gift and grain gift from us. He would not have shown us all these things, or let us hear these things."

JUDGES 13:22–23

Like many of us, Manoah was tempted to freak out in fear. God had just visited him, and he began to panic. Maybe he felt unworthy or maybe he was just plain scared, but either way he was certain he and his wife were about to take their last breath. But she confidently stepped in, pointing out truth that eventually calmed him down.

We all need people who can help us take a deep breath when we're scared. Who does that for you? Who are the ones who can calm you down? A friend or parent? A teacher or coach? An older brother or aunt? Are you that person for someone else? Let's find courage to speak up whenever others need to hear the truth.

God, help me be known as a truth teller!

The courage to face peer pressure

So the Lord said, "I will destroy man whom I have made from the land, man and animals, things that move upon the earth and birds of the sky. For I am sorry that I have made them." But Noah found favor in the eyes of the Lord. This is the story of Noah and his family. Noah was right with God. He was without blame in his time. Noah walked with God.

GENESIS 6:7–9

Noah had the courage to be holy when everyone around him was not. Rather than sin to be like everybody else, Noah chose to do what he knew was right in God's eyes. Noah didn't give in to peer pressure. Instead, he decided to be righteous.

That kind of choice takes bravery. It's easy to follow others into bad decisions because we want to fit in. We want to be liked. We want to hang out with those girls. And rather than stand firm in what we know is right, we give in.

Courageous girl, choose to be like Noah. Choose to be right with God rather than doing the wrong things to fit in.

God, I choose You!

Taking the First Step

They carried it to the Jordan and put their feet in the water.
(For the Jordan water floods during the time of gathering grain.)
Then the water flowing down from above stood and rose up in
one place far away at Adam, the city beside Zarethan. The water
flowing down toward the sea of the Arabah, the Salt Sea,
was all cut off. So the people crossed beside Jericho.
JOSHUA 3:15–16

Think of the bravery it took to step into the river when the waters were high and fast. The Israelites were trusting while scared, believing God would stop the waters like He promised. . .and He did. The people crossed the Jordan River on dry ground.

Sometimes we have to take the first step before God shows up. We have to be the one to confront our friend or be honest with a parent. We have to say no to the party or yes to meeting with a tutor. God often asks that we trust Him enough to step out in faith. Where's God asking that of you right now?

God, I am afraid to move forward.
Will You give me courage to take the next right step?

Facing the Bullies

As he talked with them, Goliath the Philistine from Gath came out
of the army of the Philistines, and spoke the same words as before.
And David heard him. When all the men of Israel saw the man,
they ran away from him and were very much afraid.

1 SAMUEL 17:23–24

Goliath was a huge man, highly trained in combat. He had
the best armor and was very strong. Goliath had a reputation
of being a killing machine, and He wasn't afraid to brag about
it. No one wanted to face that giant in battle.

We all have Goliaths in our life, those people who taunt
us and make us feel small. Maybe it's the mean girls at school
or the neighbor down the street. Maybe it's someone online
or a teammate. It could even be someone in our own family
who is quick to say mean and hurtful things.

God is not okay with anyone bullying you. If you ask,
He'll give you strength to stand up for yourself, courage to
not cower in fear, and confidence to know the truth about
who you are.

God, help me stand strong against the bullies. I need Your help.

Fearless Trust

But David said to Saul, "Your servant was taking care of his father's sheep. When a lion or a bear came and took a lamb from the flock, I went after him and fought him and saved it from his mouth. When he came against me, I took hold of him by the hair of his head and hit him and killed him. Your servant has killed both the lion and the bear. And this Philistine who has not gone through our religious act will be like one of them. For he has made fun of the armies of the living God." And David said, "The Lord Who saved me from the foot of the lion and from the foot of the bear, will save me from the hand of this Philistine." Saul said to David, "Go, and may the Lord be with you."

1 SAMUEL 17:34–37

David knew his courage came from God and that faith enabled him to fight Goliath.

Do you trust God will give you courage to face the hard days at school and home? If not, ask God for bold faith every day.

God, help me fearlessly trust You when I'm scared.

Find Your Own Armor

Then Saul dressed David with his clothes. He put a brass head covering on his head, and dressed him with heavy battle-clothes. David put on his sword over his heavy battle-clothes and tried to walk, for he was not used to them. Then David said to Saul, "I cannot go with these, for I am not used to them." And David took them off.

1 SAMUEL 17:38–39

Just like King Saul was dressing David in his personal armor for battle, sometimes others want you to face giants like they did. Their hearts are in the right place. They love you and want to help, but their way may not be the right way for you. And that's okay.

What are you struggling with right now? Where's your battle? Is it at home? Are you fighting with friends? Are you feeling left out at school? Are insecurities keeping you from being yourself? Is someone being mean and hurting your feelings? Ask God to show you the armor He wants you to put on so you can face those challenges victoriously.

God, I'm not sure how to handle hard situations. Will You show me what to do?

keeping it simple

David put his hand into his bag, took out a stone and threw it,
and hit the Philistine on his forehead. The stone went into his
forehead, so that he fell on his face to the ground. So David won
the fight against the Philistine with a sling and a stone. He hit the
Philistine and killed him. There was no sword in David's hand.
1 SAMUEL 17:49–50

All it took to beat the ginormous giant was one stone. David
didn't need shiny armor or a massive sword. He didn't need
an army to assist him. He didn't train in kung fu or some
other martial art. He simply battled the way he knew how—
trusting God.

Finding courage to face the giant things in life comes
from God alone. It's a simple truth that takes big faith. But
that simple truth packs a powerful punch to the giants that
threaten you. Ask God to fill you so full of faith that you can
stand firm no matter what.

God, sometimes it's difficult to trust You in the hard times.
Help me remember the simple truth that You'll
give me what I need to face challenges.

Love Them Anyway

*"I say to you who hear Me, love those who work against you.
Do good to those who hate you."*
LUKE 6:27

Sometimes the last thing you want to do is love others, especially when those others are nasty and mean. But God is asking you to love them anyway. He's asking you to treat them with respect even when they're treating you with hatred. And that's not easy to do!

God wants you to take care of yourself. You don't have to be a doormat that others walk on, but you can refuse to get down to their level. That means when they spread rumors about you, you don't have to spread rumors about them. When they call you names, you don't have to call them names. But you can talk to someone you trust and ask their advice. You can find safe adults to help you manage the situation.

You aren't loving them for their benefit but for yours. It keeps your heart from being bitter and cold, and it shows others that you're a Jesus girl.

*God, I'm gonna need Your help with this!
Give me the courage to love them anyway.*

out of your comfort zone

Moses said to the Lord, "Lord, I am not a man of words. I have never been. Even now since You spoke to Your servant, I still am not. For I am slow in talking and it is difficult for me to speak." Then the Lord said to him, "Who has made man's mouth? Who makes a man not able to speak or hear? Who makes one blind or able to see? Is it not I, the Lord? So go now. And I will be with your mouth. I will teach you what to say." But Moses said, "O Lord, I ask of You, send some other person."

EXODUS 4:10–13

Sometimes doing what God is asking of you feels super scary. You worry you don't have what it takes or that it will make others dislike you. You may even question if you're actually hearing God's voice at all.

But God asks us to step out of comfort zones all the time, and He will equip us to obey. Ask for the courage to say yes!

God, give me courage to trust You as I say yes to what You're asking of me.

The Fear of Rejection

About three o'clock Jesus cried with a loud voice,
"My God, My God, why have You left Me alone?"
MATTHEW 27:46

We've all felt the pain of rejection. Few things hurt more than when your friends turn their backs on you or when you don't get the invite to the big birthday party. It stings when you don't get picked for the team or others talk behind your back. Unfortunately, rejection is something we will all face from time to time.

But how comforting to know that Jesus faced it too. That means He completely understands how bad it feels. He is able to relate when your feelings are hurt. So, courageous girl, you can talk to Jesus about it because He gets it.

Take a minute and tell Him how you're feeling. Let Him know where you're struggling and where you've been hurt. Tell Him your self-doubts. Ask Him to bring comfort and peace and to give you courage to love yourself.

God, I'm glad You understand how much rejection hurts.
It makes me doubt my goodness. Please give me
strength to know I am lovable.

when God Builds, the Enemy Tries to Destroy

Those who were building the wall and those who carried loads did their work with one hand, and held something to fight with in the other hand. Each builder wore his sword at his side as he built.

NEHEMIAH 4:17–18

When Nehemiah and the others were rebuilding the wall around Jerusalem, the local people didn't want it to happen. They wanted the city to stay in ruins. But God had other plans and sent Nehemiah to secure the wall.

The truth is that whatever God builds, the Enemy tries to destroy. That's why we work with one hand and hold a weapon in the other. The best weapon available to us is the Bible. There's power in God's Word because it teaches us how to overcome the hard things we face. It encourages us when we feel down, and it reminds us of how much we're loved. It gives us courage.

When the devil tries to keep you down and discouraged, you can always find hope by reading the Bible. God will meet you there every time.

God, thank You for the Bible. Your Word is powerful!

The Power to Save

"My God sent His angel and shut the lions' mouths. They have not hurt me, because He knows that I am not guilty, and because I have done nothing wrong to you, O king." Then the king was very pleased and had Daniel taken up out of the hole in the ground. So they took Daniel out of the hole and saw that he had not been hurt at all, because he had trusted in his God.

DANIEL 6:22–23

Even all alone and surrounded by hungry lions, Daniel was saved from certain death. The cats thought their next meal was going to be an easy one, but it wasn't. An angel shut their mouths, and Daniel survived the night.

This story shows the mighty power of God to save us. He is the ultimate authority and His will, will be done. Even more, when we trust God with our situation, He will show up.

Where do you need God right now? Are you struggling in a relationship? Are you full of anger at something unfair? Find the courage to trust God sees you and will save you.

God, I need You to save me!

JUST MAKING SURE

Then Gideon said to God, "Do not let Your anger burn against me for speaking to You once again. Let me make one more test with the wool. Let it be dry only on the wool. And let the ground be wet all around it." God did so that night. For it was dry only on the wool. And all the ground was wet around it.

JUDGES 6:39–40

❮❮🌿

Gideon wanted to make double-sure he heard God right, so he boldly asked God to reconfirm the truth a second time. The Lord was gracious enough to meet Gideon's request.

This story reminds us that we can confidently ask God for clarity. We can ask Him to tell us again or in a different way. . .just to be sure. If you think God is asking you to do something, it's okay to double-check.

What's God asking that you need to confirm before moving forward? Is He opening or closing a door? Is His Holy Spirit giving you a gut-check about a decision? Be brave and ask God to verify, and He will.

God, I'm just making sure that I've heard You right. Will You tell me again?

simply unshakable

Then Caleb told the people in front of Moses to be quiet. And he said, "Let us go up at once and take the land. For we are well able to take it in battle." But the men who had gone up with him said, "We are not able to go against the people. They are too strong for us."
NUMBERS 13:30–31

Caleb wasn't about to back down. He knew God had given them the land, so the size of the people there didn't worry him. He wasn't afraid of them because he trusted God and believed Him. Even when others in the scouting party felt afraid and overwhelmed, Caleb did not. His faith in God was simply unshakable.

It's easy to be afraid when you look at problems ahead. So often, they look too big or too scary, and you don't feel safe. Instead of trusting that God will help you, you check out. You quit. You give up. But what if you decided to have Caleb-like faith instead—the kind of faith where you knew God wouldn't let you fall? You'd be simply unshakable.

God, You're bigger than any problem I face. I believe it!

Even When Things Don't Make Sense

Then God said to Abraham, "As for Sarai your wife, do not call her name Sarai. But Sarah will be her name. And I will bring good to her. I will give you a son by her. I will bring good to her. And she will be the mother of nations. Kings of many people will come from her." Then Abraham fell on his face and laughed. He said to himself, "Will a child be born to a man who is 100 years old?"

GENESIS 17:15–17

Can you imagine laughing at God? Abraham was so caught off guard by this crazy promise of a child at his age that he couldn't help but fall down and giggle. But God is in the business of doing things that don't make sense.

What that means for you is that you can ask God for the big things. You can ask for things that seem absolutely impossible and unrealistic. Not only can He answer your prayer, but so often He does! Be bold and fearless in your requests, but at the same time be prepared to trust His answers no matter what.

God, I'm believing You for big things!

obeying even when you don't feel like it

Joseph awoke from his sleep. He did what the angel of the Lord told him to do. He took Mary as his wife.
MATTHEW 1:24

Joseph learned his soon-to-be wife, Mary, was pregnant. Because they weren't yet married, he knew the baby was not his. The angel's visit revealed that Mary was carrying baby Jesus. In faith, Joseph chose to obey God and take Mary as his wife. He may not have felt like it, but he had the courage to obey anyway.

Sometimes it takes everything you have to do as you're told. Your parents may have rules you think are silly, and your teacher may be stricter than she needs to be. Coaches and leaders may require things from you that feel confining. But these rules are in place to protect you.

As long as it doesn't hurt you emotionally or physically, there are benefits to obeying even when you don't feel like it. All throughout the Bible, God blesses those who obey. When you honor those in authority, God honors you as well.

God, give me the courage to obey my parents and other trusted adults.

sorta-kinda faith

Peter said to Jesus, "If it is You, Lord, tell me to come to You on the water." Jesus said, "Come!" Peter got out of the boat and walked on the water to Jesus. But when he saw the strong wind, he was afraid. He began to go down in the water. He cried out, "Lord, save me!" At once Jesus put out His hand and took hold of him. Jesus said to Peter, "You have so little faith! Why did you doubt?"
MATTHEW 14:28–31

Peter was all in. He was ready to step out of the boat and walk on water. But once he did—once he saw the waves and the wind—his faith sank. And so did he.

It's easy to have sorta-kinda faith, where we trust God until our situation gets hard or scary. The truth is that it takes courage not to doubt when the circumstances look doubtful. And sorta-kinda faith won't hold up when life gets messy, because we'll take our eyes off Jesus.

Ask for courage to trust God no matter what.

God, make me brave so I don't have sorta-kinda faith. I don't ever want to doubt You!

Be a Bold Follower

The Lord turned and looked at Peter. He remembered the Lord had said, "Before a rooster crows, you will say three times that you do not know Me." Peter went outside and cried with a troubled heart.

LUKE 22:61–62

Right before Jesus looked at Peter, He'd been denied three times by him—just as Jesus told Peter he would. Peter was scared. It was a chaotic moment when his world was turned upside down. The man he chose to follow was being taken away, leaving Peter heartbroken and afraid. Rather than stand with courage, Peter hid.

It takes guts to stand up for what you believe. It may not be popular with your classmates or teammates. They may make fun of you for being a Jesus girl. They may even call you names for believing in God. What will you choose to do?

It's normal to be afraid to be bold in your faith. We all want to be liked, and we all want to fit in. But if you ask God for courage, He'll equip you to be a proud follower of His.

God, help me be a bold follower of You!

use your voice!

Moses asked the Lord what should be done. Then the Lord said to Moses, "The daughters of Zelophehad are right in what they say. Be sure to give them their own land among their father's brothers. Give them what would have been given to their father. And say to the people of Israel, 'If a man dies and has no son, then give what belongs to him to his daughter.'"

NUMBERS 27:5–8

Talk about bold! Back in the day, it was normal for the sons to inherit their father's land when he died, while daughters were left poor and penniless. But these five stood in front of Moses and pleaded their case, fearlessly asking for their dad's land since there were no brothers. Without God's stepping in, Moses' approval, and their voices, they would've been left with nothing.

Be encouraged! Your voice matters! And you can fearlessly fight for what you know is right. You can speak up for yourself and others. And when you bring God into it, He'll give you determination to bring about change. With Him, you're a powerful force for good!

God, help me stand up to things that need changing.

If You Make a Promise, Keep It

Then she made a promise and said, "O Lord of All, be sure to look on the trouble of Your woman servant, and remember me. Do not forget Your woman servant, but give me a son. If You will, then I will give him to the Lord all his life. And no hair will ever be cut from his head."

1 SAMUEL 1:11

Hannah wanted a baby so badly, she could barely stand it, so she asked the Lord for a son, promising he'd spend his life serving God. Because He loved her so, God gave her a child she named Samuel. Because Hannah loved the Lord, she kept her promise and took him to the temple to be raised.

Promises are a big deal because you're giving your word that something will or will not happen. You are making an agreement. You're guaranteeing. Be sure that if you are bold enough to make a promise, you follow through with it. It's how you grow trust with your friends and family.

God, I want to be trustworthy.
Help me be the kind of girl that keeps her word.

The Courage to Ask for Change

The woman left her water jar and went into the town. She said to the men, "Come and see a Man Who told me everything I ever did! Can this be the Christ?" They went out of town and came to Him.

John 4:28–30

This woman at the well was disliked. She'd made many bad choices that resulted in her being an outcast. But when she ran into town and spoke, she got their attention. No matter the sinful life she had lived, Jesus used her to bring others to Him.

Are you ashamed of some choices you've made? Are you afraid people won't listen to you anymore because you've screwed up? Maybe you cheated on a test or gossiped about a friend. Maybe you have been a mean girl or have been disobeying your parents. If so, let this story encourage you.

Spend some time confessing your sins to God and tell Him you want to be changed just like the woman at the well. Ask Him to let you be a light for your friends and family.

God, I'm boldly asking You to change my heart to love You and others more.

The Courage to Lead

*Now Lappidoth's wife Deborah, a woman who spoke for God,
was judging Israel at that time. . . . She sent for Barak the son of
Abinoam from Kedeshnaphtali, and said to him, "The Lord, the God
of Israel, says, 'Go to Mount Tabor. Take with you 10,000 men from
the sons of Naphtali and Zebulun. . . .'" Then Barak said to her,
"I will go if you go with me. But if you do not go
with me, I will not go."*

JUDGES 4:4, 6, 8

Deborah was respected in a time when women weren't valued
for their wisdom, courage, or leadership skills. She served as a
prophet and judge to Israel, and both men and women looked
to her for guidance. Even Barak, an army general, wouldn't go
into battle without Deborah by her side. What a great example
of girl power!

Deborah said yes when God put her in a leadership
position. She may not have had all the answers, but Deborah
knew God did. She trusted Him and allowed Him to use her
in mighty ways. Where is God calling you to lead?

*God, give me the courage to be a leader in
my school and my community!*

The courage to ask for more

When she came to Othniel, she talked him into asking her father for a field. When she got down off her donkey, Caleb said to her, "What do you want?" Achsah answered, "Give me a gift. You have given me the land of the Negev. Give me wells of water also." So Caleb gave her the wells in the high-land and in the valley.

JOSHUA 15:18–19

Caleb's daughter had courage to ask for more. Achsah was confident enough to step out in faith and push the limits, and it worked in her favor.

Do you ever settle for something rather than ask for more? Maybe you want a deeper friendship or more friends. Maybe you want to be on a different team or move from band to choir. Maybe you'd like to be class president rather than secretary. And rather than speak up for yourself, you allow insecurities to shut you down. If you don't ask, it may never change.

Tell God your heart's desire, and then boldly ask Him for what you really want.

God, it's scary to be brave. Will You help me be confident enough to step out?

overcoming fear with faith

*Then Mary said, "I am willing to be used of the Lord. Let it happen
to me as you have said." Then the angel went away from her.*
LUKE 1:38

The angel Gabriel had just told Mary she was going to be
pregnant with Jesus. Rather than run away scared or say no,
she said, "I am willing." Can you even imagine how scared she
must have been? She was going to grow a big baby belly for
all to see, and she wasn't even married. She must have worried
what others would think or if anyone would believe that God
planted the baby inside her. What a scary situation!

But Mary trusted even though she was afraid. She sub-
mitted to God's plans for her, and she decided that fear would
not get the best of her. She chose faith instead.

Where is God asking you to trust Him rather than give
in to worry? What's keeping you from it?

*God, sometimes what You ask of me is scary.
Make me brave so my faith is bigger than my fear.*

course correction

The angel of the Lord found Hagar by a well of water in the desert on the way to Shur. He said, "Hagar, you who serve Sarai, where have you come from and where are you going?" And she said, "I am running away from Sarai, the one I serve." Then the angel of the Lord said to her, "Return to your boss. Put yourself under her power."
GENESIS 16:7–9

Going back to serve under Sarai was the last thing Hagar wanted to do. It wasn't comfortable, and she wanted out. She didn't want to stay with that family one more second. But that's exactly where God wanted her because He had a plan.

Sometimes God asks us to do things we don't understand. We think we have a better way. Rather than trust God has an awesome outcome in the works, we go our own way. But God has a reputation for correcting our course when we make the wrong turn.

Think about it. Is God asking you to go one way but you're going the opposite direction? What would it look like to trust Him?

God, give me the guts to follow You!

Pass It On

I remember your true faith. It is the same faith your grandmother Lois had and your mother Eunice had. I am sure you have that same faith also.

2 TIMOTHY 1:5

Timothy's faith was passed down to him through his mother and grandmother. Their family obviously had a long line of faithful women who benefited so many. Not only was it a family blessing back then, but Timothy is known as a pillar—an important person—in the faith and continues to encourage us even today.

Make a decision right now to pass your faith on to those around you. Choose to make a difference by living a life of faith and trust, and find the courage to make the hard choices that will encourage others to do the same. Be the kind of girl whose life points to God in heaven.

What lifestyle changes need to happen? Ask God for the courage it will take to be all in with your faith and for the determination it will take to walk it out. With His help, you can do it!

God, let me be the reason my friends and family know God. I want to make a difference!

The Real Deal

Then Jesus said, "Someone touched Me because I know power has gone from Me." When the woman saw she could not hide it, she came shaking. She got down before Jesus. Then she told Jesus in front of all the people why she had touched Him. She told how she was healed at once. Jesus said to her, "Daughter, your faith has healed you. Go in peace."
LUKE 8:46–48

This woman was so sick, and she had been for twelve years. She'd spent all her hope and money on doctors who couldn't fix her, and she was at the end of her rope. When she heard Jesus was passing through, she laced up her sandals and headed out to find Him. She had enough faith to believe Jesus was the answer. She touched His coat and was instantly healed.

Jesus is the real deal. He isn't some cute storybook character who magically makes things happen. He isn't a made-up person for weak people to believe in. Jesus is real. He is alive. And He is always available when you need help and healing.

Confidently reach out today and tell Him what you need.

God, I believe in You.

courageous choices

A woman came with a jar of perfume. She had given much money for this. As Jesus ate, she poured the perfume on His head. When the followers saw it, they were angry. They said, "Why was this wasted? This perfume could have been sold for much money and given to poor people." Jesus knew what they were saying. He said to them, "Why are you giving this woman trouble? She has done a good thing to Me."
MATTHEW 26:7–10

Sometimes the things you do for God don't make sense to the world. Choosing His way is often very different than going along with the crowd. And because you're deciding to live differently, others may make fun of you for it. They may call you lame or say you're a prude. They may criticize you and joke about your faith. What will you do if that happens?

Just like the woman pouring her expensive perfume on Jesus' feet, your decisions may be questioned. But God will see every courageous choice and will bless you for it.

God, give me courage to not care what others think of my faith. Help me choose You every time.

The Courage to Confess

The snake said to the woman, "No, you for sure will not die! For God knows that when you eat from it, your eyes will be opened and you will be like God, knowing good and bad." The woman saw that the tree was good for food, and pleasing to the eyes, and could fill the desire of making one wise. So she took of its fruit and ate. She also gave some to her husband, and he ate.

GENESIS 3:4–6

We will make colossal mistakes in our lifetime. We will believe the wrong thing or trust the wrong people. We will choose what we think is right and will learn it wasn't. And we'll even face decisions we know are wrong and disobediently say yes anyway. Yep, we will royally mess up!

But that's not the end of the story. Because of Jesus, you can confess those bad choices and be forgiven. It will take courage and humility to admit your failures, but God isn't expecting perfection from you. He loves you, and nothing can ever change that.

God, thank You for not expecting perfection. I confess that I make mistakes. Thanks for forgiveness!

God Is the Promise Keeper

Then the Lord visited Sarah as He had said and did for her as
He had promised. Sarah was able to have a child and she gave
birth to a son when Abraham was very old. He was
born at the time the Lord said it would happen.
GENESIS 21:1–2

God made a promise to Abraham. He promised a son to him
and his aging wife, Sarah. And at the ripe old age of one hun-
dred, he became a father. The seemingly impossible promise
came to pass, and Isaac was born.

Trusting for something that seemed so out of the question took a whole lot of faith. It would have been easier to
not believe. Who wants to hope for something that probably
won't happen? But God is in the business of the impossible.
He is the ultimate promise keeper, which means you need to
be in the business of fearless faith.

What are you trusting God for right now that feels
hopeless? How can you strengthen your faith to believe?

God, help me hold on to Your promises
even when they feel impossible.

The Pressure to Be Beautiful

*Jacob loved Rachel. So he said, "I will serve you seven years for your
younger daughter Rachel." Laban said, "It is better that I give
her to you than to another man. Stay with me." So Jacob
worked seven years for Rachel. It was only like
a few days to him, because of his love for her.*

Genesis 29:18–20

Jacob fell in love with Rachel and asked her father to let them
marry. Laban agreed as long as Jacob worked for him the
next seven years. So he did. But Laban tricked Jacob, and he
unknowingly married Leah, the oldest daughter. She wasn't
as pretty as Rachel, so Jacob agreed to work another seven
years for Rachel's hand. And while it's okay that Jacob fell
in love with one sister and not the other, it must have been
hurtful to Leah.

There's a whole lotta pressure to be beautiful. And it's
often an impossible standard to reach, much less maintain. It
can leave you feeling unlovable. But you are your own kind of
beautiful. Be brave enough to embrace it.

God, I am beautiful in my own way.
Give me the courage to believe it.

Time to Let Go

She was going to have a baby, and she gave birth to a son.
When she saw that he was beautiful, she hid him for three months.
But the time came when she could hide him no longer. So she took
a basket made from grass, and covered it with tar and put the
child in it. And she set it in the grass by the side of the Nile.

EXODUS 2:2–3

The baby is Moses, and his mother was Jochebed. The pharaoh in Egypt was paranoid the Hebrew slaves were going to outnumber his people, so he ordered their newborns to be killed. Jochebed kept Moses hidden until she couldn't hide him anymore. And when the time came, she put together a plan to save his life. That courageous act allowed Moses to then go on to save the lives of millions.

There are times God calls us to let go of people we care about because He has different plans. It might be a friendship, a team, or someone else. Ask God to show you His will so you can stay in it.

God, give me courage to trust You.

Trusting God in the Crazy

So the people called out and the religious leaders blew the horns.
When the people heard the sound of the horns, they called out
even louder. And the wall fell to the ground. All the people
went straight in and took the city.

JOSHUA 6:20

The battle plan God downloaded to Joshua to take the city of Jericho was crazy by most standards. It involved walking in circles, blowing horns, and screaming. Rather than usual weapons like swords, arrows, and knives, the Israelites' weapon was obedience. The city would be theirs if they obeyed.

God doesn't think like we do. His ways are not our ways. And sometimes what He's asking sounds absolutely crazy. But find the courage to obey anyway. Choose to trust God in the crazy.

What's God asking of you that seems unusual or silly? Is He asking you to befriend the new kid or try a new sport? Is He asking you to step out of a group or spend more time volunteering? Be brave and say yes to God. Then watch what happens next!

God, I don't always understand You,
but I will always trust You.

More Great Books for Courageous Girls Like You!

100 Extraordinary Stories for Courageous Girls
Girls are world-changers! And this deeply inspiring storybook proves it! This collection of 100 extraordinary stories of women of faith—from the Bible, history, and today—will empower you to know and understand how women have made a difference in the world and how much smaller our faith (and the biblical record) would be without them.

Hardback / 978-1-68322-748-9 / $16.99

Cards of Kindness for Courageous Girls:
Shareable Devotions and Inspiration
You will delight in spreading kindness and inspiration wherever you go with these shareable *Cards of Kindness*! Each perforated page features a just-right-sized devotional reading plus a positive life message that will both uplift and inspire your young heart.

Paperback / 978-1-64352-164-0 / $7.99

The Bible for Courageous Girls
Part of the exciting Courageous Girls series, this Bible provides complete Old and New Testament text in the easy-reading New Life™ Version, plus insert pages featuring full-color illustrations of bold, brave women such as Abigail, Deborah, Esther, Mary Magdalene, and Mary, mother of Jesus.

DiCarta / 978-1-64352-069-8 / $24.99